mlr

Marxist Left Review

Number 26 – Spring 2023

Editor
Omar Hassan

Editorial committee
Mick Armstrong
Sandra Bloodworth
Omar Hassan
Louise O'Shea

Reviews editor
Alexis Vassiley

© Social Research Institute

Published by Socialist Alternative
Melbourne, October 2023

PO Box 4354
Melbourne University, VIC 3052

www.marxistleftreview.org

marxistleftreview@gmail.com

Contributions to *Marxist Left Review* are peer-reviewed

ISSN 1838-2932
rrp. $20

Subediting and proofing
Tess Lee Ack
Diane Fieldes

Layout and production
Jaan Schild
Oscar Sterner

Cover
Jaan Schild

Printed by IngramSpark

Marxist Left Review is a theoretical journal published twice-yearly by Socialist Alternative, a revolutionary organisation based in Australia.

We aim to engage with theoretical and political debates on the Australian and international left, making a rigorous yet accessible case for Marxist politics. We also seek to provide analysis of the social, political and economic dynamics shaping Australian capitalism.

Unless indicated otherwise all articles published reflect the views of the individual author(s).

We rely on our readers' support to continue publication.
You can help by subscribing at *marxistleftreview.org*

mlr

Marxist Left Review Number 26 – Spring 2023

FEATURES

REVIEWS

mlr

OMAR HASSAN

Editorial: Eighteen months of hard Labor

Omar Hassan is the editor of *Marxist Left Review*. He has been active in anti-fascist and Palestine solidarity work, and has written extensively on the Middle East.

J UST 18 MONTHS INTO ITS TERM and Labor is starting to wobble. While Albo's victory halo lasted longer than might have been expected, the situation has now clearly turned. Frustration with Labor's inadequate policies has now decisively replaced hostility to Morrison and the former Liberal government in the public's consciousness. A broad sense of malaise has crept in, colouring almost everything the government does.

The overwhelming factor in all this is the assault on living standards that has gone on under Labor's watch. Inflation has hit Australian workers hard, with incomes falling sharply when adjusted for inflation. The situation is much worse than the data shows, since the official cost of living metrics do not include the soaring cost of mortgage repayments due to higher interest rates. The resulting scenario of consistently falling living standards is unprecedented in modern Australian working-class history, where workers have steadily improved their living conditions in the 32 years since the last recession, albeit at increasingly slow rates.

While the government can't be blamed for the global inflation crisis, it is absolutely accountable for its response. Labor's economic policy team, led by the charmless Jim Chalmers, have deliberately chosen to sacrifice working-class living standards on the altar of macroeconomic orthodoxy. They have celebrated the achievement of a budget surplus – the holy grail of neoliberal economics – built off taxes on the booming mining industry and rising income tax on workers due to bracket creep. Meanwhile Chalmers has refused to adequately fund health, education and welfare reforms, or to commit the serious sums of money needed to regenerate public housing. In fact, because of their scandalous commitment to Morrison's stage 3 tax cuts for the rich, Labor is actually planning to cut spending on the NDIS and a host of other public services.

More fundamentally, Labor in opposition promised workers real wage rises in an attempt to relate to the cost of living issue. It has already betrayed this promise by asking the Fair Work Commission to deliver nominal wage rises below the rate of inflation and, embarrassingly, below what the court subsequently decided was fair. While union leaders are celebrating the industrial relations reforms that Labor has pushed through, there is no sense in which the laws are designed to empower workers to fight their bosses by lifting the draconian anti-union and anti-strike legislation currently on the books. Rather, they turn the dial on the rigged arbitration system one notch in favour of union lawyers. Now, with Labor looking vulnerable, it is possible that the second tranche of these pathetic reforms might be abandoned, with Albanese set to revert to his favourite do-and-say-nothing, small-target approach to politics.

Sadly for Albanese and Labor, refusing to take a position doesn't work as well when you're actually in charge. Nothing has made this clearer than the debate around housing over the last year or so. The government has been under immense pressure to address the severe housing crisis that has made finding affordable accommodation a challenge for millions. Labor's signature housing policy, trumpeted as an historic measure, is set to deliver a woeful 6,000 houses a year over the next five years. This is a vanishingly small figure that will have no impact whatsoever on prices, the liveability of our cities, or anything else. As with so much of Labor's policy, the media spectacle around the Housing Australia Future Fund was seen as more important than any substantive attempt to improve the lives of workers, students and the poor. But newspaper headlines don't help people feed, clothe and shelter their loved ones.

In the absence of policies that meaningfully address the soaring cost of living, Labor is losing support. And rightly so. A recent AFR/ Freshwater poll has Labor's primary vote at a lowly 33 percent, down from a peak of 37 percent last December. While this number seems healthy compared to social democratic parties overseas, the current figure mirrors what they achieved in the 2022 election: its worst showing since 1934. Other polls show different data, but the overall trend is clearly downwards.[1]

How this plays out is yet to be seen, but the growing discontent can express itself in all sorts of ways. The populist furore about the government's close ties to Qantas is indicative, where public anger at Labor's slavish defence of corporate interests was able to be harnessed by the Liberals in favour of the pro-market slogan of "greater competition".

The issue of immigration is set to be a flashpoint in coming years. Labor have opened the taps on migration, the benefits being the alleviation of labour shortages and allowing universities and other big businesses to make a killing on international students. The numbers are nearly triple the original forecasts, and in the absence of struggle or adequate social planning, are probably having a negative impact on wages and housing costs. Though migration is not the fundamental cause of these or any other social problems, it can be a powerful means of deflecting economic tensions onto racist terrain. Anti-migrant views are now regularly canvassed in the mainstream media and by various Liberals, despite the near universal backing that Labor's border policy enjoys from big business.

So far, the Liberal opposition has been unable to score any real victories on the politics of inflation, housing or any related matters. However there is a natural benefit to being in opposition: everything that goes wrong is someone else's fault. As such, Dutton's personal popularity is creeping up from a low base, and the gap between the two leaders has been steadily closing. As well, the resignations of popular

---

1.   Bowe 2023.

premiers Daniel Andrews and Mark McGowan compounds the sense of drift, and means the Labor Party must face future challenges without two of its most effective leaders in living memory.

Where the Liberals have gained some traction has been the referendum on the Aboriginal Voice to parliament. Thanks to their concerted opposition, a policy that Labor had initially hoped would score them easy points with progressives, like the apology to the Stolen Generations, has become a political minefield. The Liberals have achieved this feat by using a confusing and often contradictory series of arguments. To begin with, their opposition was expressed as concern and doubt as to how the Voice would function, and whether it would sufficiently empower local Indigenous communities as opposed to bureaucrats in Canberra. But their arguments have become increasingly and openly racist, graduating to Jacinta Price's open denial of the genocide suffered by Indigenous people in the colonial period. This evolution has happened as the No campaigners have picked up momentum from successive polls showing their lead growing, and the insipid nature of the Yes campaign.

The full significance of the likely No victory will only be clear in the aftermath of the referendum. But there are already lessons to be learnt. The Liberal Party has a loyal base which is highly motivated around issues of race and racism. This represents a solid third of the population who might have accepted the Voice had Dutton gone along with the token gesture, but were keen to go on the attack once a lead was given. Nothing that any of the most extreme proponents of the No side have said has given this group cause for concern; indeed the more rabid the racism, the more enthusiastic they have been in championing that side. Given the solidity of the Liberal primary vote – and their surge at a state level in Queensland and Western Australia – this hard-right approach is clearly not costing the Liberals any support.

Then there is the third of the population who are more consciously anti-racist, who stood on the side of refugees in the darkest days of the Howard years, and who overwhelmingly remain Yes voters today. They are horrified at the display of bigotry, but the official Yes campaign has made no serious attempt to mobilise these people outside of one major day of action in September. Yet the size and scope of these demonstrations, tens of thousands-strong in Melbourne and Sydney, thousands elsewhere, indicates that there is a solid base of anti-racism on which to build.

The real issue has been those in the middle, who started off as unsure or soft supporters of the Voice but turned to No more recently. These are mostly not rabid or necessarily even conscious racists, but simply people who don't follow the issues and don't care enough to find out. This softer bigotry, manifesting as disinterest in the plight of such an oppressed group, is given weight by the broader cost of living crisis which remains front and centre of most people's minds. As well, the messy realities of a political contest can make sticking with the status quo seem easier and safer. This is especially the case given the lack of ongoing public activism or campaigning around this or almost any other question of Aboriginal rights. While Invasion Day demonstrations are something of an exception, it is still the case that only a third of people support changing the date of Australia Day, let alone the abolition of any celebration of the racist Australian state.

Key to all this is that the Labor Party and its associated institutions have failed to prosecute a serious argument either in favour of the Voice or against the No camp. For decades the ALP has sided with the conservatives on race-related issues. From refugees to the NT intervention, youth crime, counter-terror laws and more, Labor's default strategy has been to duck for cover and back the racist position to avoid a polarisation. Given this history, it should be no surprise that they find it hard to challenge the Liberals when they are so out of practice. Yet their continuous retreat on the core issues is as remarkable as it is enraging. The Voice was supposed to be the first step, followed by a national treaty and truth-telling commission. Labor has now said it opposes a national treaty, the only element of the Uluru process with some possibility of leading to reparations and any semblance of self-determination. Labor and the official Yes side have refused to campaign against the clear racism on display. Each and every time the right have been criticised for their racism, the press have defended the bigots by attacking those doing the criticising. In this infuriating, topsy-turvy world, calling out racism is nasty and divisive while celebrating genocide is a legitimate opinion. The liberal media and the official Yes campaign have been just as happy to enforce this as the right; witness the criticisms of Marcia Langton and relatively small anti-racist actions organised by the left.

Alongside all this, big business, who initially indicated they would support the Yes campaign when they thought it would be an easy PR win, have quietly retreated. Neither the AFL nor the NRL used their finals series to back the Yes side, nor have any of the major supermarkets, airlines or other capitalist behemoths seriously intervened. The left should not expect or particularly demand such support from capital, but it is important to reflect on the cynical impotence of bourgeois anti-racism.

Overall then, the Voice has brought some of the dynamics of global politics to Australia. It has given the hard right a focus around which to build, and exposed the inability of the political centre to respond to this terrible development. Whether the right can continue to make gains following the referendum is unclear, but this whole experience is a clear indication of the need to build a socialist alternative to the reformist and centre-left forces. It is a problem that this stark situation has been so misread by the tiny groups and individuals around the "progressive No" campaign. By failing to comprehend the central dynamic of the referendum and respond appropriately, they have in practice provided useful cover for the bigots. Emblematic of this has been Indigenous Senator Lidia Thorpe's attempts to reach out to the racist No side, offering to work with Warren Mundine and Jacinta Price on multiple occasions.

Foreign policy is perhaps the only field where Labor is enjoying a clear run, on the basis that they are aggressively championing the cause of US imperialism in the Pacific region. Foreign Minister Penny Wong has been on an endless tour of the various island nations, holding out the carrots of aid and work visas in exchange for joining Team America. Labor has also given the green light to turn Australia's north into an American military outpost, where it is highly likely that nuclear weapons are now being deployed alongside B52 bombers. And while "budget constraint" has been Jim Chalmers' phrase of choice, the government has renewed its support for acquiring nuclear attack submarines. This outrageous decision makes Australia's involvement in a war with China more likely, will cost the taxpayer upwards of $400 billion and will tear a gaping hole in the global non-proliferation treaties surrounding nuclear technology.

Paul Keating and Bob Carr, experienced attack dogs for the Labor Right, briefly galvanised opposition to AUKUS, albeit on an objectively pro-imperialist and nationalist basis. Their talking points – that the money could be better spent on other weaponry and that war with China was not in Australia's interest – have dominated the anti-war sentiments expressed in the mainstream and on the broad left. This manifested briefly within the ALP itself, centred on sections of the party with anti-nuclear traditions, notably the Electrical Trades Union. But after early success in passing an anti-AUKUS motion at the Queensland state conference, the machine quickly turned the screws to prevent the members "embarrassing" their leadership. For a party with such a long imperialist history, preparing for war with China and maintaining the US alliance are not up for discussion.

As is often the case under Labor governments of late, there has been little left-wing opposition to any of Labor's right-wing agenda. The remnants of the old anti-war movement have been unable to mobilise more than a few hundred people, so too those campaigning for the 13,000 refugees languishing on inhuman bridging visas that need to be renewed every six months.

On the core issue of inflation and living standards, only the union leaders are in a position to act. But the current batch seem largely content to run our movement into the ground. Strikes and union density are at historic lows, and there is no prospect of a turnaround. It is historically unprecedented for union membership and activity to be declining at a time of full employment and high inflation. It is even worse when you consider the fact that growing numbers of young workers are increasingly hostile to the rich and open to left-wing ideas.

Under Adam Bandt the Greens have consistently positioned themselves as a clear left opposition to the ALP. They have consciously sought to fill the social democratic space Labor once occupied on issues of welfare, healthcare and education. Most recently, it was housing where they made their biggest splash. By holding up the government's legislative agenda for months, the Greens were able to put renters' rights on the map for the first time in many decades. This stood in stark contrast to their earlier approach in waving through Labor's mild rebranding of Tony Abbot's climate policy. Yet just as the public had been won to policies once seen as radical, such as rent caps, the Greens capitulated, despite Labor making no changes to the appalling status quo for renters. So overall then, despite rhetorically shifting left, the Greens remain a loyal opposition to the ALP. As Eleanor Morley wrote in *Red Flag*:

> The Greens have developed their own rhythm in tandem with the government. First, they criticise proposed legislation for not going far enough. Next, they pass it anyway, amid claims that they extracted great concessions. Finally, they insist they will keep fighting, despite having lost all leverage.[2]

The various failures of the moderate left, the radicalisation of the mainstream right, and the growing economic and political tensions all point to the need to build a socialist movement in this country.

References

Bowe, William 2023, "Voting Intention", *Poll Bludger*. www.pollbludger.net/fed2025/bludgertrack/

Morley, Eleanor 2023, "The Greens capitulate on housing", *Red Flag*. redflag.org.au/article/greens-capitulate-housing

---

2.   Morley 2023.

MICK ARMSTRONG

From Marx to Lenin: Debates that forged the socialist approach to war

Mick Armstrong is the author of numerous pamphlets and articles on revolutionary organisation and the Australian labour movement.

I N AN ERA OF INTENSIFYING IMPERIALIST TENSIONS between the US and China, an accelerating arms build-up by all the major powers and the growing threat of all-out war, in part foreshadowed by the current brutal war in Ukraine, it is worth looking back at the debates among socialists in the lead-up to and during the First World War. It was out of those at times furious debates, literally in the heat of battle, that the Marxist approach to imperialism and the struggle against war was forged. The economic and political realities today are, of course, not entirely the same. The imperialist pecking order has changed substantially, most notably in recent decades with the rise of China. The destructive capacities of the competing militaries have been qualitatively enhanced with the development of nuclear weapons which threaten the very existence of the planet. Nonetheless the vital insights developed by Lenin, Luxemburg, Trotsky, Bukharin and other revolutionaries of that earlier period of rising imperialist contention and eventual world war still provide sound foundations upon which socialists can build.

The 4th of August 1914 was a decisive turning point for the socialist movement. The collapse of the great majority of parties of the Second Socialist International into pro-war chauvinism and support for their own ruling classes laid the basis for a fundamental divide in the socialist movement between reformists and revolutionaries, leading to the eventual founding in March 1919 of the Third Communist International – the Comintern.

The capitulation of these supposed Marxist parties, above all the German Social Democratic Party (SPD), the leading party of the Second International, was the product of a long-term degeneration and accommodation to the capitalist system by the leadership of the parties and their associated trade unions. It was not simply a question of a mistaken position on war policy or militarism but reflected a broader integration into the capitalist system, and an increasing identification with their own nation state. This dynamic was most pronounced among the trade union leaders and a cohort of MPs and party functionaries. Well before 4 August these leaders had abandoned the interests of their working-class followers and crossed over to the side of the bourgeoisie. The debates in the socialist parties about war, colonial policy, militarism and imperialism which occurred in these years were but one reflection of that broader capitulation – though a most decisive one.

Marx and Engels on war

The original Marxist approach to war developed by Marx and Engels occurred in a period prior to the rise of modern capitalist imperialism. Marx and Engels saw war as an abomination that was part of the very essence of capitalism and previous class societies. It was only with the overthrow of capitalism and the development of a socialist world order that war could be eliminated. The First International, formed in 1864, in which Marx and Engels played a leading role, denounced standing armies as an incitement to militarism and championed instead the concept of the popular militia with officers democratically elected. They believed that a popular militia would be less amenable to being used by governments to crush strikes and working-class revolts.

Marx and Engels supported the victory of the rising capitalist powers in their wars against semi-feudal reaction, drawing a parallel with the wars of revolutionary France against the old feudal powers, backed by England, which sought to crush the great revolution. In particular they supported wars against tsarist Russia which they saw as the backbone of reaction in Europe. At the time of the 1848 revolutionary wave that swept Europe they called on the forces of democracy to wage a revolutionary war against tsarism. They believed that the defeat of tsarism would speed up the coming proletarian revolution. Over subsequent years they continued to call on England and the other powers to wage war on tsarism.

Marx and Engels also supported wars of national reunification in Italy and Germany. They supported the North against the slave-holding South in the US Civil War and the armed national rebellions in Ireland and Poland. They believed these were progressive wars that would hasten the development of capitalism and put workers in a better position to fight for freedom.

In wars between capitalist powers Marx and Engels supported the principle of national defence. In the 1870–71 Franco-Prussian war that culminated in the 1871 Paris Commune, Marx and Engels took a concrete tactical approach based on their assessment of whose victory best served the interests of the revolutionary cause. At the outbreak of the fighting they supported a defensive war by Prussia, which they hoped would precipitate the downfall of the reactionary Bonapartist French regime. After the fall of Bonaparte they opposed the Prussian invasion of France and went on to support the defence of Paris by the popular forces of the National Guard.

Marx and Engels' general attitude to war was appropriate until roughly the 1880s, when the rapid development of imperialist competition demanded a new approach. It is debatable exactly when the modern imperialist system was consolidated, but it definitely had been by the beginning of the twentieth century. In a world increasingly carved up by the imperialist powers, the principle of national defence had been made redundant for the likes of Britain, France, the US and Germany. Indeed talk of national defence was now a reactionary concept in any war between the imperialist powers. By the early 1890s Engels sensed an important change had occurred and warned of the threat of a reactionary Europe-wide war which could devastate the continent and derail the development of the working-class movement. However there was a considerable delay before socialists developed an approach to war appropriate for the modern imperialist epoch.

Even Lenin, later vital to the development of a Marxist theory of imperialism, long held to elements of the old approach. Seeing tsarist Russia as the main enemy, in 1904 Lenin supported the defeat of Russia by Japanese imperialism, which he argued was a progressive force. In January 1905 he expressed delight at the fall of the Russian garrison at Port Arthur, regarding "progressive", "advanced" Asia as having dealt an irreparable blow to old, "reactionary", "backward" Europe.[1] This approach of advocating the defeat of reactionary tsarism, even if by other imperialist forces, still coloured Lenin's standpoint at the outbreak of World War I.

The road to capitulation

In the early 1900s a number of Marxist theorists, including Rudolph Hilferding and Rosa Luxemburg, began to develop analyses of the new capitalist imperialism and an opposition to imperialist war.[2] The resolution against war adopted at the 1907 Stuttgart conference of the Socialist International and reaffirmed in 1910 at Copenhagen and again in 1912 at Basel, implicitly (but only implicitly) broke with the old Marx and Engels approach. It proclaimed that the socialist parties should stridently oppose the outbreak of war:

> Should war break out none the less, it is their duty to intervene
> in favour of its speedy termination and to do all in their power
> to utilise the economic and political crisis caused by the war
> to rouse the peoples and thereby to hasten the abolition of
> capitalist domination.[3]

A worthy declaration is one thing; more important, however, is what is done in practice. The Second International was not a centralised body but a federation of national parties that held Congresses roughly every three years. The individual national parties were not mandated to carry out the decisions of those Congresses. An International Socialist

---

1.   Lenin 1905.
2.   Hilferding 1981 (first published in 1910), and Luxemburg 2003 (first published in 1913).
3.   Gankin and Fisher 1940, p.59.

Bureau was established as an executive of the International in 1900 but its decisions were also only recommendations. The International developed no clear guidelines for collective action to fight militarism and no common program when war erupted. Thus for example at the special Basel Congress of the International in November 1912, called in response to the outbreak of the Balkan Wars, there was plenty of maximal rhetoric and strident attacks on capitalist imperialism, but no definite strategy was adopted for opposing the drive to war.

On the extreme left of the Socialist International, Domela Nieuwenhuis of the Netherlands as early as 1891 had called for socialists to launch an armed insurrection in response to war. This call was later championed by French socialist Gustave Hervé, but with the outbreak of World War I Hervé flipped from this bombastic ultraleftism to an extreme French chauvinism. Then at the 1907 Stuttgart conference the old French Blanquist and Communard Edouard Vaillant, with the support of British Independent Labour Party leader Keir Hardie, moved an amendment calling for a general strike if war broke out. However revolutionaries like Lenin and Luxemburg recognised that the anarchist-style approach of Hervé was unworkable. A general strike or insurrection can't be summoned on command at the best of times, let alone in the face of nationalist euphoria provoked by a declaration of war. As for talk of a general strike by reformists like Hardie, that was dismissed as hot air. The right-wing socialists also naturally denounced calls for a general strike or other forms of militant action. They did not want to commit to *any* concrete measures against war.

Little in the way of practical activity to lay the basis for concerted opposition to war was developed by the Second International parties, despite a prolonged arms race in the early twentieth century. This was to a considerable part due to the approach of the leadership of the German SPD, easily the most influential party in the International. The young radical Karl Liebknecht did commence an anti-militarist campaign in Germany in 1904, publishing his crusading polemic *Militarism and Anti-Militarism* in 1907.[4] Liebknecht received support

---

4. Liebknecht 1973.

from SPD youth groups in radical centres such as Stuttgart but he was stomped on by the party leadership at the 1906 Mannheim Conference.[5]

There were a few other examples of anti-war agitation by the international left. In France the syndicalist-led trade union federation, the General Confederation of Labour (CGT), which was not affiliated to the Socialist International, to its credit did for some years concertedly campaign against militarism and conscription. But it too gradually began to make its peace with the capitalist system, and like the French Socialist Party capitulated at the outbreak of war. In 1905 the Swedish Social Democrats called on workers to launch a general strike if the government carried out its threat to invade Norway after it declared independence from Sweden. In Italy the Socialist Party expelled right-wing supporters of the Italian invasion of Libya in 1912. In Australia the small socialist movement campaigned against so-called "boy conscription" in the pre-war years, with some activists being jailed.[6] However these were exceptions that went against the grain of the International's passivity.

From about 1907 the SPD increasingly accommodated to German nationalism and colonialism. The right-wing revisionists in the party opposed abolishing the colonies as a "utopia" and claimed that German imperialism was a progressive force bringing "European civilisation" to the colonies. Edward David, a leading revisionist, argued at the 1907 Stuttgart Congress of the International that "Europe needs colonies. It does not have enough of them". The revisionists in turn were backed by the powerful trade union leaders. Opposition to colonialism was only narrowly carried by a vote of 127 to 108 at the Stuttgart Congress, with SPD delegates making up much of the pro-colonial minority.[7] The International never clearly declared that "defence of the fatherland" did not apply to imperialist war, and even sections on the SPD left in these pre-war years still clung to the concept of national defence. Much of the SPD left and the international far left in this period backed pacifist appeals for international disarmament and for an international court of arbitration to settle disputes between the Great Powers. These

---

5. Schorske 1955, pp.69–70, 72–5 and Trotnow 1984, pp.55–71.
6. For the campaign against "boy conscription" see Barrett 1979 and Jauncey 1968.
7. Riddell 1984, pp.6, 15.

utopian reformist positions were voted up unanimously at the 1907 Stuttgart Congress of the International, though in 1911 Rosa Luxemburg polemicised against such pacifist illusions in her article *Peace Utopias*.[8]

One of the first serious tests came with the 1911 Morocco crisis, when the German navy cruiser *Panther* sailed into Agadir harbour in a direct challenge to France's imperialist interests in North Africa. The centrist SPD leadership did not want to speak out, fearful of an electoral backlash. But in the major German cities where the SPD left was strong protests were organised and the central leadership were eventually forced to back the protests after Luxemburg exposed their prevarication. The Morocco crisis did not only expose the backsliding of the SPD. The Socialist International took no initiative. It was entirely passive in the face of the war threat – a clear sign of what was to come.[9]

Then in April 1913, in a secret meeting of the budget committee of the German Reichstag, the Social Democrats present did not protest when the army's plans for an offensive in the west at the beginning of a war were revealed to them. In the same year, after a heated debate in its parliamentary caucus, the SPD for the first time voted to support new taxes to fund increased arms spending, using the excuse that the money was to be raised by an income tax rather than indirect taxes that disproportionately hit workers and the poor.

The problem, however, was not just the right wing of the socialist movement. In 1912 Karl Kautsky, the most prominent socialist theorist of the day and a leading representative of the SPD centre, abandoned his previous opposition to any war by the German state, whether offensive or defensive. Where he had once argued that socialists could not make a meaningful distinction between the two, Kautsky now backed party leader August Bebel's support for any supposedly defensive war by Germany. Kautsky argued that no proletariat could remain indifferent to the fate of the nation in the event of invasion.[10]

Kautsky also began to develop his theory of ultra-imperialism, which he argued could supersede the imperialist phase of capitalist development. Kautsky claimed that the increasing economic

---

8.   Riddell 1984, pp.71–75.
9.   Schorske 1955, pp.197–205.
10. Salvadori 1990, p.176.

integration of capitalist industry across national borders and the massive expansion of world trade and investment made a full-scale war unlikely. It would be more profitable, he argued, for the emerging giant capitalist monopolies to peacefully divide up the world between themselves rather than to support wars by rival nation states. A rehashed version of this economic determinist theory was put forward in recent decades by the autonomist Toni Negri, and in more recent times these ideas have been used to dismiss the danger of war between the US and China.[11]

Kautsky polemicised against the argument made by the SPD's revolutionary left that "war is strictly linked to the essence of capitalism".[12] He claimed that rearmament was not an economic necessity of capitalist development, but was rather the result of a specific economic policy due to the weight commanded by particular forces in the state. Kautsky claimed that only a few sectors of capital, above all finance capital and the arms manufacturers, supported war and that they could potentially be disciplined by the dominant sections of the industrial capitalist class that had no interest in conflict.[13] This, in his view, opened up the possibility of an alliance against war between socialists and progressive capitalists. It was therefore necessary "to support and strengthen the movements of the petty bourgeoisie and bourgeoisie against war and the world arms race".[14] To aid these developments socialists should in turn focus on campaigning for arms control and the arbitration of international disputes. Even after the outbreak of World War I, the greatest slaughter in human history, had decisively refuted his argument that a peaceful capitalism was possible, Kautsky published an article arguing:

> There is no *economic* necessity for continuing the arms race after the World War, even from the standpoint of the capitalist class itself, with the possible exception of certain armaments interests.

---

11. Hardt and Negri 2000. For a critique of Negri see Callinicos 2001.
12. Salvadori 1990, p.171.
13. Nation 2009, p.17. See Lenin 1973, pp.142–8 and Bukharin 1972 pp.130–43 for contemporary critiques of Kautsky's ultra-imperialism.
14. Salvadori 1990, p.171.

On the contrary, the capitalist economy is seriously threatened precisely by these disputes. Every far-sighted capitalist today must call on his fellows: capitalists of all countries unite![15]

Well before the war the most militant section of the SPD left and of the Socialist International around figures like Rosa Luxemburg had developed a more rigorous critique of imperialism. However the lefts tended to concentrate their fire against the right-wing revisionists and did not clearly differentiate themselves from the Kautskyite centre. Compounding the problem was the fact that the reactionary nature of Kautsky's standpoint on imperialism was not immediately obvious even to a committed anti-militarist like Karl Liebknecht, who associated himself with Kautsky's position at the SPD's 1912 Chemnitz Congress.[16] It was only in the aftermath of the SPD's 1913 Jena Congress that Luxemburg, who was the clearest, called for "a systematic offensive against the swamp [the Kautskyites]".[17] As well, the lefts were hampered by the fact that most of them viewed party unity as sacrosanct and feared splits. The lefts also opposed a centralised international that might have been able to discipline the reformists. So the major political differences in the socialist movement were fudged until the war broke out. It has to be said that in the pre-war years even Lenin, despite his harsh criticisms of the German revisionists, still saw them as a legitimate shade in the International. Lenin also still had illusions in Kautsky and did not seriously attempt to organise an international left on clear lines. So while Lenin had split from the Menshevik reformists in Russia, he did not generalise that approach to the whole of the International, even though the reformists in Germany, Austria and France were in a series of ways politically worse than the Mensheviks.

As the imperialist powers edged closer to war, the socialist parties, despite their strong working-class support bases in the major European states, were largely passive. They did not politically prepare their ranks to stridently combat the virus of nationalism. Reflecting how far they had accommodated to bourgeois society, many of the reformist

---

15. Riddell 1984, p.180.
16. Salvadori 1990, pp.177–8.
17. Riddell 1984, p.97.

leaders right up until the very outbreak of the war clung to illusions in the peaceful intentions of their own ruling classes. Bruce Glazier, a leader of the left reformist British Independent Labour Party, was still claiming in July 1914 that the "whole of the [British] cabinet wants peace". Leading French socialist Jean Jaurès declared in a speech on 29 July 1914: "the French government wants peace and works to maintain peace. It is the best ally of the peace efforts of the splendid British government". On 30 July 1914 the SPD's Berlin daily paper *Vorwärts* proclaimed that the German Emperor Wilhelm II "has proved himself to be a sincere partisan of international peace".[18] Meanwhile the Austrian socialist leader, Victor Adler, had thrown up his hands in despair and abandoned any pretence of mounting resistance to the war drive. Having passively accepted the build-up to war it was no great leap for the leaders of the major parties to go over to outright support for their own nation once the war had been officially declared.

Adding to the pressure to capitulate was the surge of middle-class pro-war hysteria, the threat of harsh repressive measures that would destroy the unions, the parties and all the working-class institutions built up in peaceful times. By 1914 the German SPD had a million members, an apparatus that employed 10,000 people and investments of 20 million marks in its various enterprises, all of which were threatened if the party was outlawed.[19] Thus the SPD could go from organising mass demonstrations against the threat of war in July 1914 to unanimously voting for war appropriations only a couple of weeks later, following the declaration of war on Russia. The German workers who had heroically defied police violence to protest in huge numbers against the war were left totally abandoned by their leaders. The SPD left, paralysed by their commitment to party unity and discipline, offered no alternative.

The SPD's capitulation had a profoundly demoralising impact on socialist-inspired workers right across Europe. The party that had been held up as the beacon of hope for workers, the party that other smaller socialist parties had aspired to emulate, had now betrayed. In Russia militant workers, who in the face of savage police repression and brutal

18. Riddell 1984, pp.116–19.
19. Carsten 1982, p.17.

assaults by middle-class mobs had been striking and protesting against the war, were thoroughly disoriented when the news came through of the SPD's vote for war credits.

The opportunists sought to cover up their warmongering with a left-wing gloss and came up with an array of theoretical justifications for their betrayals. In voting for war credits the SPD Reichstag faction declared that Germany was fighting a war of self-defence and pathetically hoped that the war would be ended "by a peace which makes friendship possible with neighbouring peoples".[20] The opportunists in Austria and Germany also dredged up Marx and Engels' hostility to tsarism. A German victory, it was claimed, would advance the interests of workers in both Russia and Germany by provoking a revolution to overthrow tsarism. In France and Britain leading socialists declared that they were fighting a defensive war against reactionary Prussian militarism. That wasn't a total lie; the war was a defence of their ruling classes' colonial conquests from the rising power of Germany.

Most of the leaders of the centre in the SPD and the other socialist parties backed the initial vote to support the war, but were somewhat shamefaced about it. As the war dragged on and working-class discontent increasingly surfaced, sections of the centre began verbally to drift to the left to cover their tracks. They began to talk of a "democratic peace", of a negotiated settlement "without victors or vanquished" and to reject annexations. In June 1915 Kautsky, Haase and even Bernstein of the SPD came out for a negotiated peace. Later, after being driven out of the SPD by the vitriolic pro-war right, they found themselves on the right wing of the centrist Independent Social Democratic Party (USPD).

Debates on the revolutionary left

The scale of the betrayal by the leading parties of the Socialist International left the small bands of socialists that held firm to internationalist principles shocked and initially extremely isolated. Lenin at first refused to believe reports that the SPD had voted for war credits. The revolutionaries were confronted with the task of

---

20. Rosdolsky 1999, p.35.

developing a thoroughgoing critique of imperialism and socialist opportunism, combined with a strategic and tactical approach to the struggle against the war. "The result", in R Craig Nation's words, "was one of the most intense and creative debates in the entire history of socialist thought, a debate about alternative visions of revolutionary transformation in the circumstances of the twentieth century".[21] There was a flourishing of theoretical work, including important works on imperialism – Lenin's *Imperialism, the Highest Stage of Capitalism* and Bukharin's *Imperialism and World Economy*.[22] These debates are of ongoing relevance in light of the sharp accentuation of imperialist rivalry between the US and China.

The revolutionary left all agreed on three key points: first, that this was an imperialist war that had to be opposed by workers in all the combatant countries; second, that the leaders of the social democratic parties had betrayed the working class; and third, that a workers' revolution was needed to end the war and the whole system of capitalism that bred wars. However there was a series of at times strident debates: over revolutionary defeatism, the peace slogan, the disarmament slogan, national liberation struggles and the need for a clear break with the reformists and centrists to form a new revolutionary socialist international.

Lenin rightly spent the early years of the war establishing a hard-left pole of attraction that made no concessions to opportunists, and combated any illusions about achieving peace without workers' revolutions. He sought to draw a sharp line between revolutionaries and pacifists who believed the war could be ended on just terms through negotiations.

Revolutionary defeatism is commonly held up as the core element of Lenin's opposition to the imperialist war. However he used the term much less frequently than is commonly portrayed, and even before he arrived back in Russia in the wake of the February 1917 revolution he had dropped talk of defeatism. Prominent Bolsheviks disagreed with Lenin on the defeatism slogan, and not just waverers or more conservative figures such as Kamenev. The left of the party around

---

21. Nation 2009, p.59.
22. Lenin 1973, Bukharin 1972.

Bukharin, Krylenko, Piatakov and Bosch also opposed it.[23] Zinoviev was one of the few leading Bolsheviks who backed Lenin. In terms of the activity of Bolshevik militants on the ground in Russia during the war years revolutionary defeatism seems to have played little or no role. According to one study:

> A textual analysis of forty-seven leaflets and appeals published illegally by Bolshevik militants between January 1915 and 22 February 1917 is most illuminating. Not a single leaflet mentioned the essential Leninist slogan of the defeat of Russia being the lesser evil.[24]

Virtually nobody on the international revolutionary left, including Trotsky, Luxemburg and Radek, supported revolutionary defeatism.[25] As Rosa Luxemburg argued in *The Junius Pamphlet*:

> For the European proletariat as a class, victory or defeat of either of the two war groups would be equally disastrous. For war as such, whatever its military outcome may be, is the greatest conceivable defeat of the cause of the European proletariat. The overthrow of war and the speedy forcing of peace, by the international revolutionary action of the proletariat, alone can bring to it the only possible victory.[26]

The Communist International in its early revolutionary years did not adopt revolutionary defeatism in relation to imperialist wars. Revolutionary defeatism was only revived in 1924 as a cynical manoeuvre by the troika of Zinoviev, Kamenev and Stalin in their campaign against Trotsky and as part of their authoritarian drive to "Bolshevise" the Comintern and crush all revolutionary opposition.[27]

---

23. See for example the declaration of the left Bolshevik Baugy group, Riddell 1984, pp.250–1.
24. McKean 1990, p.361.
25. For detailed critiques of the revolutionary defeatist slogan see Draper 1953/54, Pearce 1961 and Rosdolsky 1999.
26. Waters 1970, p.323.
27. Draper 1953/54 and Joubert 1988.

The Sixth Comintern Congress in 1928 fully installed defeatism and it subsequently was turned into a dogma by the Stalinists.

Lenin changed his position a series of times on what revolutionary defeatism concretely meant and flip-flopped back and forth between substantially different meanings of the slogan. At the outbreak of the war he supported the military defeat of Russia by German imperialism, which he saw as the lesser evil compared to reactionary tsarism – essentially Marx's old position. Bukharin pointed out that this was effectively the same position as the German SPD leadership which also backed a German military victory using a similar justification. Lenin retreated in the face of this criticism to a position that workers not only of Russia but of every belligerent country "must not falter at the possibility of that country's defeat".[28]

Lenin began to call on socialists to take a position of revolutionary defeatism in all the contesting powers, though he explicitly ruled out the use of sabotage of the war effort. He also briefly argued that "wartime revolutionary action against one's own government means not only desiring its defeat, but really facilitating such a defeat".[29] Later he changed his stance again, stating that all revolutionary defeatism meant was that socialists should not hold back the class struggle out of fear of jeopardising the imperialist war effort of their government. This, however, was no different from the position of Trotsky, Luxemburg, Radek and co., whom he had sharply criticised earlier.

As Trotsky pointed out, socialists could oppose the war and support working-class mass action to confront capitalism without embracing the confusing slogan of revolutionary defeatism – ie supporting the victory of the opposing imperialist army over your own ruling class. Trotsky described Lenin's formulation as "defencism turned inside out" and as "social patriotism standing on its head".[30] In his 1914 pamphlet, *The War and the International,* Trotsky argued:

> We must not for a moment entertain the idea of purchasing the
> doubtful liberation of Russia by the certain destruction of the

28. Riddell 1984, p.252.
29. Lenin 1915a.
30. Quoted in Pearce 1961.

> liberty of Belgium and France, and – what is more important still
> – thereby inoculating the German and Austrian proletariat with
> the virus of imperialism.[31]

It was undoubtedly necessary for revolutionary Marxists to draw a sharp line between themselves and reformists and centrists who hid behind pacifist slogans to disguise their unwillingness to back mass working-class struggle to end the war. That objective, however, could be achieved without embracing the ultra-radical sounding but disorienting slogan of revolutionary defeatism.

The last time Lenin publicly raised the defeatism slogan was in November 1916. Back in Russia in April 1917 Lenin recognised that the Bolsheviks were not going to win over the mass of workers and soldiers by proclaiming maximalist slogans. The working masses wanted peace, but they also feared that a German military victory would result in the defeat of the Russian revolution. Indeed by September 1917 sections of the Russian bourgeoisie hoped for a German invasion to crush the Bolsheviks.

Lenin also changed his position on the peace slogan. At the start of the war he stridently polemicised against the peace slogan and counter-posed to it the slogan of "turn the imperialist war into civil war". "Not 'peace without annexations'", he proclaimed, "but peace to the cottages, war on the palaces; peace to the proletariat and the toiling masses, war on the bourgeoisie".[32] In a letter to Radek he denounced "the obtuse and traitorous slogan of peace".[33] Lenin saw the call for peace raised by centrists like Kautsky as being in direct opposition to a workers' revolution which was the only way to end the war. As he wrote in a letter to his fellow Bolshevik Shlyapnikov: "The watchword of peace, in my opinion, is incorrect at the present moment. It is a philistine, parson's watchword. The proletarian watchword must be civil war".[34]

Lenin rightly pointed out that in a capitalist world the only peace possible was an "imperialist peace" based on the balance of

---

31. Trotsky 1914.
32. Lenin 1916.
33. Nation 2009, p.78.
34. Lenin 1914. See also Lenin 1915a.

forces between the Great Powers. Lenin attacked Kautsky's call for a "democratic peace" as a utopian demand which simply created illusions in the imperialist governments and deflected from the need for revolutionary struggle. The reformist leaders claimed they were for a "democratic peace" that involved the renunciation of all annexations and war reparations. But this simply meant supporting the pre-war imperialist status quo – the existing division of the spoils of empire.

On similar grounds Lenin opposed calls for universal disarmament and the international arbitration of disputes that had been unanimously adopted at the 1910 Congress of the Second International and which was still advocated by sections of the revolutionary left. The Norwegian and Swedish Socialist Youth League, which was an important component of the Zimmerwald left, continued to be influenced by this pacifist position. Universal disarmament, however, is impossible under imperialism, and even if capitalism was overthrown in one or two countries, the new workers' states would need to be armed to defend themselves. As well, Lenin rightly argued that socialists should not demand the disarmament of colonial and nationally oppressed peoples. Unlike many on the revolutionary left, including Luxemburg, Radek and Bukharin, Lenin backed armed national rebellions in colonies such as Ireland and India and by the oppressed nations of the Russian empire. He understood that those national revolts could play an important role in challenging capitalist rule. As for international arbitration, in a class-based society there was no genuinely neutral body capable of justly settling disputes, and any decision would merely reflect the balance of imperialist forces.

Lenin was correct to argue that talk of a democratic peace, disarmament and the like was utopian under capitalism. War could only be ended under socialism. It was undoubtedly true that Kautsky and co. were raising these slogans in opposition to a strategy of working-class struggle to end the war and the capitalist system that bred it. But that did not entirely settle the issue. As discontent rose over the collapse of living standards, food shortages, falling wages, incredibly harsh working conditions, conscription, the slaughter at the front and the crushing of democratic rights, workers and the mass of the oppressed increasingly demanded peace. Revolutionaries could not turn their backs on those demands. As Trotsky wrote in August 1916 in criticism of Lenin's approach:

> [E]xperience shows that the mobilization of proletarian opposition everywhere has taken place precisely under this slogan [the struggle for peace]. Only on this basis can revolutionary internationalists today successfully carry out their work. The formula of *civil war* expresses in an essentially correct way the inevitable exacerbation of all forms of class struggle in the coming period. But they [the Bolsheviks] counterpose it to the struggle for peace, which causes the formula to hang in mid-air and lose its meaning for the period we are going through.[35]

Workers were not demanding peace out of cynical pro-imperialist motivations but out of heartfelt concerns. They were not looking to prop up capitalism. The Bolsheviks in their agitation in the factories could not simply denounce calls for peace as utopian. That would have cut them off from the masses they needed to win over and driven them back into the arms of the opportunists. Once he was back in Russia Lenin clearly recognised this. The Bolsheviks could not simply proclaim: "Turn the imperialist war into a civil war" to the millions who were yearning for peace and an end to the war. It was way too maximal. Lenin now criticised the previous Bolshevik orientation, with its insistence on hard formulations, as too theoretical and abstract an approach:

> The masses take a practical and not a theoretical approach to the question. We make the mistake of taking the theoretical approach...
>
> We Bolsheviks are in the habit of taking the line of maximum revolutionism. But that is not enough. We must sort things out.[36]

More concrete demands and transitional slogans were necessary

---

35. Quoted in Riddell 1984, p.405.
36. Lenin 1917a.

that constructively related to mass sentiment and sought to move it forward in a revolutionary direction. The Bolsheviks' practical program became: no class peace; no participation in war-time governments; no war credits; carrying out illegal work; and encouraging fraternisation at the front between troops of the opposing armies. The key Bolshevik slogans for the October Revolution famously became "Bread, Peace and Land", combined with the means to achieve these goals: "All Power to the Soviets".

This concrete program was a product of the tactical flexibility of Lenin and the Bolsheviks as they applied their principled revolutionary politics to the realities of the class struggle and the emerging consciousness of the working masses as they moved towards revolutionary conclusions. Maximalist ultimatums were of no use. Revolutionaries had to patiently win workers to a series of transitional steps that led to them ultimately taking power.

In the aftermath of the February revolution the Bolsheviks were confronted with another vital issue – what Lenin called the "honest defencist" sentiments of many soldiers and workers.[37] These soldiers believed it was necessary to fight on, not for the imperialist goal of seizing territory, but to protect the gains of the revolution. The Bolsheviks did not retreat at all from their determined opposition to the war, but they had to relate to these genuine concerns.

The Bolsheviks did not call for mutinies in the army or desertions from the front. The war would not be ended by soldiers simply "sticking their bayonets in the ground" or abandoning the front – that was pure demagogy, an anarchist or pacifist idea. The war could only be ended by revolutions in several countries. The first step would be for workers and soldiers to take power in Russia. In the short term that meant forming soldiers' soviets, fraternisation with the enemy and opposing reckless offensives ordered by the Provisional Government that sacrificed thousands of lives in pursuit of an imperialist agenda of territorial conquests. In a similar vein, in May 1917 Lenin called on the peasants to seize the land, but added that they should do so "using every effort to increase the production of grain and meat since the

---

37. Lenin 1917b.

troops at the front are in dire straits".[38] The point here is that individual refusal to work or fight was no step forward: the socialist solution to these immense problems could only be found through collective action and the democratic transformation of society.

This approach was soon to be tested. In the months before the October revolution top tsarist officers conspired to open the front for the Germans to capture St Petersburg. And as John Reed recorded:

> A large section of the propertied classes preferred the Germans to the Revolution...and did not hesitate to say so. In the Russian household where I lived, the subject of conversation at the dinner table was almost invariably the coming of the Germans, bringing "law and order"... One evening I spent at the house of a Moscow merchant; during tea we asked the eleven people at the table whether they preferred "Wilhelm or the Bolshevikii". The vote was ten to one for Wilhelm.[39]

Bolshevik-influenced troops however, such as the Lettish regiments, fought hard to prevent German advances.

Zimmerwald and a new International

As an internationalist Lenin was not narrowly focused on developments in Russia during the war years. With the collapse of the Second International into support for the war Lenin immediately came out calling for a new revolutionary international. At the start of the war the forces of the revolutionary left were far too small to make that a practical proposition. Small openings for the revolutionary left emerged in March and April 1915 at the International Conference of Socialist Women and the International Socialist Youth Conference, which were both to the left of the mainstream of the Socialist International. At the women's conference Inessa Armand pursued what was to become the broad tactical orientation of the Bolsheviks at a series of international left conferences: "challenging the dominant moderate consensus but striving to avoid an open breach". Their goal was "to use the conferences

---

38. Lenin 1917c.
39. Reed 1961, p.7.

as a platform to air an alternative viewpoint, to recruit supporters and to exert some influence on the final resolutions".[40]

The women's and youth conferences helped lay the basis for the first serious step forward for the anti-war left, the September 1915 Zimmerwald conference in Switzerland. The bulk of the small group of attendees at Zimmerwald did not advocate revolutionary struggle to end the war. They mostly held centrist-style positions, and did not see themselves as laying the basis for a new International. The key figure behind the Zimmerwald movement, Robert Grimm of the Swiss Socialist Party, stood for "class struggle not civil truce" but he was not a revolutionary and opposed splits in the socialist parties. The conservative wing of Zimmerwald was represented by figures such as the SPD parliamentarian Georg Ledebour who, although he was to the left of Kautsky, had up to this point voted for war credits. Ledebour and the left Menshevik Martov were for restoring the International around the common denominator of peace.

Even some more left-wing delegates, such as Trotsky, the Romanian, Christian Rakovsky, who went on later to become a leading Bolshevik, and Vasil Kolarov, subsequently a leader of the Bulgarian Communist Party, did not join the Zimmerwald left bloc that Lenin laboriously fought to cohere. In a few cases this was because they did not want at this stage to totally cut off their links with the Second International. Trotsky, for example, despite having a thoroughly revolutionary standpoint in opposition to the war, still held onto illusions in the possibility of unity of Russian socialists. Recognising this reality, Lenin in the lead-up to Zimmerwald had toned down his conditions for affiliation to the left bloc to: (1) unconditional condemnation of opportunism and social chauvinism; (2) a revolutionary action program (with the concession that whether one preferred the slogan "mass strike" or "civil war" was of secondary importance); (3) refutation of defence of the Fatherland.[41] Notably this program did not call for revolutionary defeatism or a break with the Second International and the foundation of a Third International. Nor did it call for support of struggles for

---

40. Nation 2009, p.69.
41. Nation 2009, p.83.

national self-determination which significant figures in the left bloc, such as Radek, still opposed.

The Zimmerwald manifesto, which was drafted by Trotsky, was a compromise. It raised the democratic peace slogans and did not call for a revolutionary civil war. The Zimmerwald left voted for the manifesto as they saw its call to struggle as a step forward. Nonetheless they publicly criticised it for saying nothing critical about the socialist opportunists and for not offering a clear pronouncement about the methods for fighting against the war.[42]

Zimmerwald played an important role in reviving the spirit of the anti-war left and the first minimal steps had been taken in establishing a left bloc of revolutionary opponents of the war. By the time of the second conference of the Zimmerwald movement in April 1916 at Kienthal, also in Switzerland, the tide had shifted substantially to the left, with an upsurge of working-class protests and strikes over the appalling deterioration of living standards, incredibly long working hours, food shortages and the never-ending war. The resolution on peace adopted at Kienthal was more radical than the Zimmerwald one, with a call for the overthrow of the capitalist class, a more explicit call for a vote against war credits and a description of arms controls and compulsory arbitration of international disputes as mere utopias. The actual Kienthal manifesto, however, did not fully reflect this shift and the issue of breaking with the Socialist International was still fudged. The right wing had threatened to walk out of the conference if a vote to split from the International Socialist Bureau was carried.

The arguments of the left bloc organised by Lenin were gaining a broader hearing as events unfolded and the class struggle increasingly broke out. The Zimmerwald left, despite an ongoing lack of cohesion, was increasingly critical of the socialist centre and was pulling in new forces including Giacinto Serratti, the editor of the Italian socialist paper *Avanti!*, three Swiss delegates and a prominent Serbian socialist. The basis was being laid for the formation of the Communist International. The revolutionaries' argument that the war could be ended by working-class revolts was to be decisively proved correct

---

42. Lenin 1915b.

over the next two years by the October 1917 revolution in Russia, the November 1918 German revolution and a series of further revolts that swept across Europe and much of the world.

Conclusion

The fundamental principles of the Marxist approach to war and imperialism developed in response to World War I have substantially stood the test of time. Socialists must oppose both sides in all wars between imperialist powers, support the mobilisation of mass opposition to such wars and stand for ending war and the capitalist system that breeds it by working-class revolution. Lenin's strategic orientation of "turn the imperialist war into a civil war" remains correct.

It is not enough, however, to make abstract calls for a revolutionary challenge to imperialism. Militant action against militarism and war is vital. Socialists also need to develop specific slogans and transitional demands that can help galvanise opposition to any specific war and assist workers to draw the conclusion that they need to overthrow capitalism. Socialists have to relate to all the partial struggles of workers and the oppressed around the issues of falling living standards, the deterioration of wages and working conditions, the undermining of democratic rights and racist scapegoating brought on by the war, as these can help to lay the basis for a powerful anti-war movement. Maximalist rhetoric should not be counterposed to calls for peace, opposition to preparations for war and the basic defence of living standards, especially when those calls are not the cynical rhetoric of opportunist politicians but arise from the mass of workers and the oppressed. The specific slogans socialists raise will necessarily depend on the concrete political circumstances of the day. They will be significantly different in a period leading up to war, like the present, and the period after the actual outbreak of shooting.

One important modification of the Marxist approach to war has been necessitated by the development of nuclear weaponry. Nuclear weapons are qualitatively different from conventional weaponry in their destructive capacity. Unlike rifles or machine guns, they are not weapons that the working class or a workers' state can simply turn against the bourgeoisie. Indeed, an all-out nuclear war would threaten the very destruction of our planet and the entire human race. For these reasons socialists should definitely campaign for nuclear disarmament. In countries which already have nuclear weapons the demand of socialists must be the unilateral nuclear disarmament of their own ruling class. In countries, like Australia, which don't currently have nuclear weapons, socialists should stridently oppose any move by their ruling class to acquire them.

As in 1914, there is in the world today no neutral or independent body that can be looked to for the just arbitration of disputes between the imperialist powers or prevent the spread of nuclear weapons. The United Nations, to which many liberals and pacifists appeal to prevent wars, has been utterly ineffective. The UN is after all a gathering of our enemies – the ruling classes of the world. The UN Security Council is dominated by the major imperialist powers and, as has been shown repeatedly, if one of the major powers, such as the US, cannot get its way on the Security Council it will act unilaterally. Mass action remains the only option to challenge the drive to war, and the threat of war can ultimately only be ended by workers taking power out of the hands of the capitalist classes of the whole world.

References

Barrett, John 1979, *Falling In. Australians and "Boy Conscription" 1911–1915,* Hale & Iremonger.

Bukharin, Nikolai 1972 [1915/1917], *Imperialism and World Economy,* Merlin. https://www.marxists.org/archive/bukharin/works/1917/imperial/

Callinicos, Alex 2001, "Toni Negri in perspective", *International Socialism,* 2:92, Autumn. https://www.marxists.org/history/etol/writers/callinicos/2001/xx/toninegri.htm

Carsten, FL 1982, *War against War. British and German Radical Movements in the First World War,* University of California Press.

Draper, Hal 1953/54, "The Myth of Lenin's 'Revolutionary Defeatism'". https://www.marxists.org/archive/draper/1953/defeat/index.htm

Gankin, Olga Hess and HH Fisher 1940, *The Bolsheviks and the World War. The Origin of the Third International,* Stanford University Press.

Hardt, Michael and Antonio Negri 2000, *Empire,* Harvard University Press.

Hilferding, Rudolf 1981 [1910], *Finance Capital. A Study of the Latest Phase of Capitalist Development*, Rutledge and Kegan Paul. https://www.marxists.org/archive/hilferding/1910/finkap/

Jauncey, LC 1968, *The Story of Conscription in Australia*, Macmillan.

Joubert, Jean-Paul 1988, "Revolutionary Defeatism", *Revolutionary History*, 1 (3), Autumn. https://www.marxists.org/history/etol/revhist/backiss/vol1/no3/revdeft.html

Lenin, VI 1905, "The Fall of Port Arthur". https://www.marxists.org/archive/lenin/works/1905/jan/14.htm

Lenin, VI 1914, "Letter to AG Shlyapnikov". https://www.marxists.org/archive/lenin/works/1914/oct/17ags.htm

Lenin, VI 1915a, "The Defeat of One's Own Government in the Imperialist War". https://www.marxists.org/archive/lenin/works/1915/jul/26.htm

Lenin, VI 1915b, "The 'Peace Slogan' Appraised", *Collected Works*, Vol.21. https://www.marxists.org/archive/lenin/works/1915/jul/x01.htm

Lenin, VI 1916, "Peace Without Annexations and the Independence of Poland as Slogans of the Day in Russia". https://www.marxists.org/archive/lenin/works/1916/feb/29.htm

Lenin, VI 1917a, "Report at a meeting of Bolshevik delegates to the All-Russian Conference of Soviets of Workers' and Soldiers' Deputies", 4 (17) April. https://www.marxists.org/archive/lenin/works/1917/apr/04d.htm

Lenin, VI 1917b, "Honest Defencism Reveals Itself". https://www.marxists.org/archive/lenin/works/1917/apr/21b.htm

Lenin, VI 1917c, "An Open Letter to the Delegates to the All-Russian Congress of Peasants' Deputies". https://www.marxists.org/archive/lenin/works/1917/may/07b.htm

Lenin, VI 1973 [1916], *Imperialism, the Highest Stage of Capitalism*, Foreign Languages Press. https://www.marxists.org/archive/lenin/works/1916/imp-hsc/

Liebknecht, Karl 1973 [1907], *Militarism and Anti-Militarism*, Rivers Press. https://www.marxists.org/archive/liebknecht-k/works/1907/militarism-antimilitarism/index.htm

Luxemburg, Rosa 2003 [1913], *The Accumulation of Capital*, Routledge. https://www.marxists.org/archive/luxemburg/1913/accumulation-capital/

McKean, Robert B 1990, *St Petersburg Between the Revolutions*, Yale University Press.

Nation, R Craig 2009, *War on War. Lenin, the Zimmerwald Left, and the Origins of Communist Internationalism*, Haymarket Books.

Pearce, Brian 1961, "Lenin and Trotsky on Pacifism and Defeatism", *Labour Review*, 6 (1), Spring. https://www.marxists.org/history/etol/writers/pearce/1961/xx/defeatism.html

Reed, John 1961 [1919], *Ten Days that Shook the World*, Lawrence & Wishart. https://www.marxists.org/ebooks/reed/ten-days-that-shook-the-world-reed.pdf

Riddell John (ed.) 1984, *Lenin's Struggle for a Revolutionary International*, Monad.

Rosdolsky, Roman 1999, *Lenin and the First World War*, Prinkipo Press.

Salvadori, Massimo 1990, *Karl Kautsky and the Socialist Revolution 1880–1938*, Verso.

Schorske, Carl E 1955, *German Social Democracy, 1905–1917. The Development of the Great Schism*, Harvard University Press.

Trotnow, Helmut 1984, *Karl Liebknecht (1871–1919). A Political Biography*, Archion Books.

Trotsky, Leon 1914, *The War and the International (The Bolsheviks and World Peace)*, https://www.marxists.org/archive/trotsky/1914/war/index.htm

Waters, Mary-Alice 1970, "The Junius Pamphlet" [1915], in *Rosa Luxemburg Speaks*, Pathfinder. https://www.marxists.org/archive/luxemburg/1915/junius/index.htm

VINIL KUMAR

Class struggle in the Pacific

Vinil Kumar is a socialist activist living in Sydney. He has written about Australian imperialism in the Pacific, and domestic politics in Fiji and the Solomon Islands.

O N 3 MARCH 1920, New Zealand's *Otago Daily Times* published a report titled "Fiji Labour Troubles" by its correspondent in Suva. It began with an observation of events in mid-February:

> Suva is practically under martial law. There is no one left in the large stores but the owners and a girl or two. Business has practically stopped. Everybody is a special constable. There is a mild excitement in the air and nervous people shut their doors at night...

> There is an Indian "strike" on.[1]

The strike in question had begun weeks earlier, following the release of Fiji's remaining Indian indentured labourers from their bondage. The end of indenture had engendered a sense of optimism and hope among Indian workers that life could get better. This newfound freedom led the governor of Fiji to decry a "certain swollen-headedness" that made Indian workers "perilously difficult to handle".[2]

On 15 January, workers at the Public Works Department in Suva

---

1. *Otago Daily Times* 1920, p.8.
2. Gillion 1977, p.19

initiated the strike, after they were informed that their working hours would be increased from 45 to 48 hours a week. Their bosses backed down the next day and invited them to return to work on their old terms, but the workers refused, declaring: "We do not get enough to satisfy our bellies".[3] They demanded a pay rise to address rising living costs and over the next week were joined by workers in the predominantly Indian Nausori and Rewa districts, one of the sites of the Australian Colonial Sugar Refinery company (CSR). Over four thousand workers in Navua, where another major sugar mill was located, also joined the strike, at a time when the population of Fiji was approximately 157,000.

Domestic servants and shop workers for European merchants who refused to join the strike were threatened and humiliated. The Indian Women's Association led crowds of women to beat up scabs who remained loyal to the bosses and the government, in a manner that the papers described as "Bolshevist".[4] When three Indian workers were put on trial in Nausori for intimidating scabs, a thousand demonstrators turned up to demand their release.

Much of the strikers' anger was directed at Europeans, reflecting the reality of their oppression at the hands of price-gouging shop owners, plantation overseers, government officials and CSR managers. One episode during the strike saw hundreds of Indians riot in Suva when a notoriously racist European hotel-owner beat his Indian servant and abused Indians passing by. The colonial administration used this anti-European sentiment, growing calls for equality for Indians and the role of Indian political organisations in the strike as proof that the strike was political and not really concerned with wages.

The authorities mobilised to crush the strike, concerned that Indian agitation could rouse sympathy and discontent among native Fijians – thus threatening the entire colonial project.[5] Practically all military-aged Europeans were armed and hundreds of native Fijians were enlisted as special constables or as strike-breaking scabs. The administration requested military aid from the Australian government, who dispatched a warship. A naval ship from New Zealand was delayed

---

3.   Gillion 1977, p.25.
4.   *Otago Daily Times* 1920, p.8.
5.   Gillion 1977, p.30.

when waterside workers refused to load a ship in solidarity with the strikers in Fiji.

The strikers defended themselves with sticks and stones, and sabotaged roads and telephone lines. One worker was killed after police ambushed a group heading into Suva to procure supplies. Just over a month after it began, the strike was brought to an end. This was, in part, due to the efforts of a wealthy Indian planter and nominated member of the Legislative Council who secured a return to work and the banishment of one of the strike's key agitators.

The strike had a lasting impact and caused a political crisis for the colonial administrations in both Fiji and India. As a result, some concessions to the strikers were made and the strike eventually led to Indians in Fiji being able to elect their own parliamentary representatives for the first time. Fijian labourers in the sugar industry sympathised with the strikes and also began to demand higher wages for themselves, and even the scabs brought in by CSR began to turn against the company after experiencing what it was like to work for them.[6] The strike also paved the way for a six-month shutdown of the sugar industry the next year.

Stories like these clash with the idyllic image of the Pacific, a tropical oasis seemingly separated from the history of class struggle seen elsewhere in the world. But as capitalism spread itself across the globe, "creating a world after its own image", it brought with it a new kind of society built on the exploitation of workers for the production of wealth. The history of capitalism in the Pacific, like the history of capitalism and class society everywhere, is the history of class struggle.

This article seeks to unearth some of the key struggles that took place in Fiji, Papua New Guinea and the Solomon Islands during the twentieth century. The particular episodes chosen provide useful lessons for socialists everywhere in understanding and fighting the international capitalist system, as well as attesting to the fighting spirit of rebels across the Pacific. This history also crucially rebukes postcolonial criticisms of Marxism that dismiss its relevance to the

---

6. Gillion 1977, p.59–60.

global south, and instead illustrate why Marxism is the only theory that can provide a coherent account of this hidden history.

Capitalism in the Pacific

The history of the modern Pacific can't be understood separately from the history of imperialism. As capitalism developed in Europe, the most industrialised powers became locked into competition with each other, expanding their reach globally and carving up the world into their own colonial empires. After the American revolution, the United States became another rival to British imperialism and Britain established a key outpost on the Australian continent. Australia developed into a regional imperialist power in its own right, albeit one that relied on a more powerful ally such as Britain or the United States to underwrite its power in the region.

The first human inhabitants had begun to settle the islands of the Pacific as early as 90,000 years ago and as late as 1200 CE. By the early 1500s, European vessels had begun to navigate the region and establish contact and trade with locals. The race to carve up the South Pacific accelerated dramatically during the nineteenth century. The Dutch had colonised Indonesia in 1799. France took control of New Caledonia, the new ruling class in Australia successfully campaigned for the British seizure of Fiji, the territory of Papua and part of the Solomons, while Germany seized New Guinea and the remainder of the Solomons.

The development of capitalism and the class forces in each Pacific Island territory were shaped by the interests and plans of its colonial power, and the social conflicts they provoked.

Fiji

After the Australian gold rush of the 1850s, the ruling class based in Victoria saw Fiji as an investment opportunity, where a profitable plantation economy could capitalise on cotton shortages caused by the American Civil War. CSR also saw the territory as suitable for its sugar plantations. But given the limited military resources Britain was willing to commit to expansion in the Pacific, colonial rule in Fiji would depend on an alliance between Australian capital and a section of Fiji's indigenous chiefs, who could help them rule the territory. For political reasons, coercing Fijians and other Pacific Islanders into plantation labour was not an option and British annexation in 1874 was cloaked in the rhetoric of protecting native Fijians.

Instead, cheap labour for Fiji's plantations would be provided by over 60,000 Indian indentured labourers who were brought to the islands between 1879 and 1917. This meant that a modern labour force was created in Fiji earlier than in any other Pacific Island country, with Indian workers becoming a core part of the agricultural and urban workforce.

Labour organisation in Fiji dates back to the 1880s.[7] The earliest strikes by Indian labourers took place in 1882 over wages and excessive work, while 1890 saw the first strike by indigenous Fijian dockworkers in Suva. In 1916, an attempt was made to organise the first formal union among indigenous dockworkers in Lautoka by a member of the Australian Workers' Union living in Fiji. European teachers and workers in the civil service also formed white-collar unions in the 1920s. Though strikes had been a feature of the sugar industry for decades, the first unions of sugar workers weren't formed until the 1940s.

Papua New Guinea

Germany sought to turn the north-eastern territory of New Guinea into a serious plantation colony for itself in the 1880s. As a major industrial power, it was better placed to do so than its Australian rival. The Australian ruling class, however, was much more interested in stopping its rivals establishing a foothold in the region. This was summed up in an editorial in the *Melbourne Daily Telegraph* in 1875, which argued: "though we do not want the island ourselves, we do want very much that no one else shall have it".[8] The success of the plantation economy of German New Guinea was cut short when the territory was seized by Australia during World War One.

The development of modern industry was limited for the first 50 years of colonial rule.[9] For example, rather than operate copra plantations themselves, companies found it more profitable to engage

---

7.   Hince 1985.
8.   *Daily Telegraph* 1875, cited in Thompson 1980.
9.   Amarshi, Good & Mortimer 1979.

small-scale peasant growers to harvest the crop, which would then be bought and processed. Industry also faced labour shortages, as native Papuans were reluctant to leave their villages and responded with hostility to attempts to coerce them into work. The Australian government itself prioritised establishing a strong colonial military and police administration that could maintain control over the territory and discipline its inhabitants. This included outlawing and suppressing attempts to organise independent unions during the colonial period. During World War Two, Australia's occupation of Papua New Guinea involved the forced conscription of native Papuans as labourers, who were beaten and tortured for disobedience[10] and some were executed for treason.[11] Despite the repressive nature of the colonial state, there were also sporadic instances of resistance, including a strike of 3,000 workers in the rural town of Rabaul in 1929.

Following the Second World War, dramatic shifts took place in the region. The collapse of the British empire, and the growth of independence movements in India and Indonesia, saw the Australian government shift to supporting independence for Papua New Guinea. This was to shape the post-independence order to best suit its own interests and included writing the country's constitution and cultivating a compliant local political class. The postwar boom also saw an increase in Australian government spending and foreign investment in the territory, fuelling the growth of industry and urban centres.

The 1950s saw welfare organisations develop among urban workers, paving the way for the first independent union to emerge in Port Moresby in 1960: the PNG Workers' Association.[12] This reflected growing discontent among new urban workers. In response, the government introduced tripartism in 1963 and a system of compulsory arbitration, resulting in the legalisation of unions and the creation of many by the Department of Labour for the purposes of arbitration. Many of these unions were run by individuals or small committees with little connection to the rank-and-file workers they represented, and were often conservatised by the anti-communist politics of the

10. Riseman 2010.
11. Close-Barry & Stead 2017.
12. Hess & Gissua 1992.

Cold War. But the legalisation of unions created space for the creation of a number of serious independent unions. These included the Public Service Association, the Teachers' Association, the Central District Waterside Workers Union which represented Port Moresby dockworkers, and eventually the Bougainville Mining Workers' Union.

Solomon Islands

From the 1820s, the Solomons became a significant transit point for sailors and traders, particularly between Asia and Australia's east coast. In the 1860s, Australia began its "blackbirding" slave trade in the Pacific, with thousands of people being taken from Vanuatu to supply plantations in Queensland with cheap labour. But by the 1870s, they were running out of people to steal, so their sights turned to the Solomon Islands, which ultimately provided around 40 percent of all blackbirding labour.[13] After Germany annexed New Guinea, it also took control of the northern Solomon Islands. To protect Australia's critical shipping routes and labour supply, Britain established control over the remaining Solomon Islands in 1893 and took over possession of the German-controlled islands in a treaty in 1899.

In the early part of the twentieth century, British and Australian firms established copra plantations across the islands. But the impact of blackbirding, the introduction of diseases and the brutality of plantation life, to which almost all able-bodied men were subjected, saw a decline in the population and a serious labour shortage. A system of indenture was used to tie labourers to their employers and a head tax was imposed from 1921 for all working-age men, requiring them to enter waged employment in order to pay it off. Tax collectors forced locals to pay up with an armed escort of police and native volunteers. The resentment of this situation is encapsulated by the 1927 killing of Australian district officer William Bell as he collected taxes on Malaita, the most populous island of the Solomons. In retaliation the Australian government dispatched the HMAS *Adelaide* on an expedition to the island.

During World War Two, Japan occupied part of the central

---

13.   Moore 2017.

Solomon Islands. They began to construct an airfield on the island of Guadalcanal but after being driven out by the Allies in 1943, the US took over the site and completed the construction of the Henderson airfield, using labourers brought over from Malaita.

These events and the end of the war led to three key interrelated developments that shaped the Solomon Islands working class.

First was the Maasina Rule movement. Contact with American soldiers during the war had a political impact on Malaitan labourers. Ian Frazer describes how the Americans "talked a lot about political and industrial rights".[14] They often paid more to Solomon Islands casual labourers and remarked on how little the British paid them, and the presence of Black and white soldiers seemingly serving in the military as equals challenged the ideas of white racial superiority that justified colonial rule. Towards the end of the war, as many labourers returned home to Malaita, the first mass political movement in the Solomon Islands was launched.

In the eight years between 1944 and 1952, Maasina Rule looked to replace the British administration which was seen to have failed the island's inhabitants with a form of Malaitan self-governance. A core part of this movement was a refusal to be recruited as labourers for the British, resulting in a serious labour shortage. They also demanded that wages be raised from £1 to £12 a month, approximately the average wage for European plantation workers. When the government tried to defy the recruitment ban in 1947, the movement's leaders called a strike of all Malaitans employed by the government and forced the government to back down. But after calling off the strike, these leaders were arrested, sparking off another round of protests. The government began a campaign of repression in 1948, reviving taxation, jailing thousands who refused to pay and strangling local food supplies. The recruiting boycott was broken in 1950 and though the movement limped on, it was finally wound up in 1952.

The second development was a shift from indentured to "free" labour. This in large part reflected a broader shift in colonial policy by the crumbling British empire, but Maasina Rule had also created a

---

14.   Frazer 1990, p.196.

crisis for the plantation economy and highlighted the political volatility of a system of coerced labour. Unions were also legalised in 1946 and the Department of Labour played a role in forming the earliest unions.

Finally, the current capital of Honiara was built around the Henderson airfield. The construction of both the airfield and the city depended largely on migratory labourers from Malaita and other islands, concentrating them for the first time into a major urban centre and creating a multi-ethnic urban working class. As most colonial spending was directed towards establishing a state administration and law enforcement, and with foreign capital only flowing into a small number of industries, the formation of large workplaces was largely limited to the civil service, plus a few select manual industries such as agriculture and shipping.

The first formal unions took shape in these two sectors in the early 1960s. The British Solomon Islands Workers Union formed in 1960, covering plantation and waterside workers, and many of its founding members had been active in Maasina Rule. Within its first six months, the union had signed up 2,000 members, representing a quarter of all waged workers in the country.

The Solomon Islands general strikes

The first of multiple general strikes in Honiara took place in October 1962 and was led by manual labourers working for the government.[15] It was in response to a discriminatory new award which gave white expatriate civil servants a 20 percent pay rise, local civil servants a 13 percent increase and manual workers 10 percent. At the end of the month, all government manual workers struck without any lead from their union; they were joined by other workers in the city and in total, over 1,100 workers remained on strike until they got the same 20 percent pay rise as the expatriate civil servants.

In September 1964, over 900 plantation workers struck for eight days against the British Levers company over pay. The company broke the strike by enlisting scabs from a minority ethnic group and dividing the workforce.

---

15. Frazer 1992.

That month, the Department of Labour split the union into one for Ports and Copra workers and one for Building and General Workers.

The BGWU immediately began wage negotiations, demanding that the basic wage be almost doubled to £15 per month. But in late March 1965, the union leadership accepted a wage offer of under £9. A week later, almost 800 government labourers and private sector workers staged an unofficial general strike throughout Honiara when they learned of their union's sellout.[16] The workers marched from Chinatown to the centre of the city, intimidating those who refused to join them on strike. After police harassed and arrested a demonstrator carrying a traditional Malaitan club, more than 300 workers marched to the central police station to demand his release. When the police chief ordered the crowd to disperse, they pelted the police with stones. In response, tear gas was used in Honiara for the first time ever. The strikes lasted eight days, grew to involve over 1,500 workers and spread to several towns on nearby islands. The government finally succeeded in breaking the strike by threatening to sack the workers and ship them back to their homes on other islands. Despite this, 20 percent of the strikers still refused to return to work and were forcibly repatriated.

Though the fortunes of these early strikes were mixed, they showed an impressive level of militancy that laid the basis for future struggles and developments in unionism. Independent unions and a new generation of union officials began to emerge in the mid-1970s and their fight for recognition led to further outbreaks of struggle.

The newly formed Solomon Islands General Workers Union set off another general strike in July 1975, this time led by stevedores working at the Ports Authority seeking to have the independent union recognised.[17] They were joined by over 1,300 other workers from across Honiara. After two weeks on strike, the workers not only won recognition for their union, they also won pay increases of between 20 and 25 percent, compensation for their time on strike, and more. It brought to prominence the union's founder Bartholomew Ulufa'alu, who would go on to become a prominent figure in Solomon Island

16. *Tribune* 1965, Moore 2022, Frazer 1992. The narrative of the 1965 strikes has been pieced together from these writings.
17. Frazer 1992.

politics. Emboldened by the strike, union leaders continued to push for union recognition with other employers, using the threat of strike action if they refused and organising at times illegal political demonstrations in Honiara. As a result six union officials were arrested and fined, including Ulufa'alu, who was imprisoned in December. But on 2 January 1976, the largest and final general strike of over 4,300 workers took place. This accounted for 70 to 80 percent of all workers in Honiara and the Guadalcanal Plains. The ensuing political crisis forced the government to intervene and resulted in union recognition by dozens of employers.

Though union militancy continued after the Solomon Islands gained independence in 1978, a number of developments posed new challenges for the working class. In 1981, the government introduced the Trades Disputes Act, which required unions and employers to engage in compulsory arbitration that took into account "the economy as a whole" and created a framework through which strikes could be declared illegal. Subsequently, wage rises were restricted to two-thirds of inflation and many unions recognised that dispute panels heavily favoured employers.

There was also the issue of aspirationalism. In a country with limited economic opportunities, leadership of unions and entry into politics presented some of the few opportunities for social mobility, particularly among the more educated. Bartholomew Ulufa'alu entered politics in 1976 and founded the National Democratic Party. But as the country's population was and remains largely rural, the potential for electoral success for parties based on workers was limited. On the one hand, this meant Ulufa'alu shifted to the right to build a broader electoral base and the Solomon Islands Labour Party which formed later could only ever manage to win a few seats. But on the other hand, this meant it was harder to present electoralism as a viable strategy for the working class. This, combined with the political impact of Maasina Rule and the struggles of the 1960s and '70s, meant that a militant tradition among some unions in the Solomon Islands endured in the following decades, most notably among teachers and nurses.

While the histories and political contexts of Fiji, Papua New Guinea and the Solomon Islands differ, a number of common themes emerge.

Firstly, imperialist expansion and the establishment of colonial rule implanted the capitalist mode of production into these countries. Even where the development of capitalist industry was limited, the logic of commodity production also began to reshape and impact those who continued to live a more traditional life. Modern bureaucratic and repressive state apparatuses had to be constructed in order for these new nation-states to be administered. Resistance in these circumstances was always inevitable, whether it be against a rising class of employers or the oppression required by colonial rule. These struggles created traditions of militancy and radicalism that would shape and be shaped by the emergence of an urban working class created by capitalism.

The 1959 oil workers' strike in Fiji

The development of capitalism in the Pacific also created an indigenous ruling class in each country. The political role of this social layer in Fiji was illustrated during the 1959 oil workers' strike.

Though a section of Fiji's chiefs agreed to the British annexation of Fiji in 1874, there were those who resisted. In the late 1860s and early 1870s, armed rebellions known as the Kai Colo waged a struggle against the colonising power, but were ultimately defeated by troops and armed settlers from Australia, and armed Fijians from the eastern regions. A Great Council of Chiefs was created in 1876 which enshrined their power as the figureheads of the colonial state.

While indentured Indians became the main source of plantation and urban labour for Fiji, a small number of indigenous Fijians also joined the workforce. But most continued to live in rural villages where traditional social structures regulated the use of land and village life, and tied them to the authority of the high chiefs allied with the colonial administration. But the fondness for the administration wasn't shared by many ordinary Fijians. An overriding sense of political domination and economic exploitation saw further resistance and a desire for self-government, a notable expression of which was the Viti Kabani (or Fiji Company).[18] This attempt at building an alternative economic

---

18. Nicole 2011.

structure to the colonial state in which rural Fijians produced and traded among themselves only lasted between 1913 and 1917, but in that time spread across virtually the entire island group.

The leasing of Fijian land, first to plantation owners who employed Indian labour and then later to freed Indian labourers becoming farmers, created the basis for friction between the two groups. But in the wake of Indian labour militancy which the colonial administration feared could inspire solidarity from indigenous Fijians, a conscious effort was made to divide the groups. William Sutherland notes of the 1920 strike:

> State and capital feared that Fijian sympathy for Indian workers might make the upheavals more generalized. By dissuading Fijians from supporting the strikers and by ranging Fijian policemen and special constables against them, the ruling class manipulated the basic antagonistic relationship between capital and labour so as to make it appear racial.[19]

The colonial government positioned itself as protector of indigenous Fijian society from Indians who were supposedly coming to steal and grow wealthy off their land and leave them in poverty.

During World War Two, Indians refused to fight under the banner of the British empire and for a government that denied them political equality. Instead, in 1943 strikes swept the cane-growing regions. This provoked a racist backlash from the establishment, who decried the subversive and disloyal Indian population. European hotelier JJ Ragg addressed parliament in 1946, denouncing the "great increase in non-Fijian inhabitants" and advocating for Fiji to be "kept as a Fijian country".[20] These events and arguments laid the basis for Fijian ethnic chauvinism in the following decades, couched in the language of "indigenous rights".

Unlike their Indian counterparts, indigenous Fijians served in the war and after it ended, economic conditions forced many to migrate to urban centres in search of work. The shift weakened their identification

---

19. Sutherland 1992, p.52.
20. Sutherland 1992, p.62

with village life, as they began to forge new common interests as part of a Fijian and Indian urban workforce, many of whom were under the thumb of European employers.

In the late 1950s, new cost of living pressures began to bite and demands for higher wages emerged. The Wholesale and Retail Workers General Union (WRWGU) was formed in 1958 and among its early leaders were Apisai Tora, a returned Fijian soldier who had been radicalised by the experience of the war, and James Anthony, of Indian-Irish-Polynesian background, who had been influenced by the son of Australian Communist Party unionist "Big Jim" Healy, Kevin Healy, who was living in Suva at the time.

The union covered oil workers at Suva's depots for Shell and Vacuum Co. In late 1959, the union put forward a claim for the weekly wage to be almost doubled to £6 per week, and demanded a 40-hour working week, sick leave and two weeks' paid vacation. After the company responded with a minuscule pay rise and nothing else, Anthony notified the companies of a strike on Monday 7 December at the Suva Depot, as well as at Nadi airport and Vuda Point.

Workers picketed at all three depots. The strike meant that within 24 hours, fuel supply to the country ran low, causing disruption to international flights at Nadi airport and food supply. The water-pumping station and power plant at Tamavua were only spared on Anthony's insistence that supplies to essential services be maintained and that workers be "law abiding". The next day an oil tanker unloaded fuel for distribution at Vuda Point under police escort. A European clergyman forced his way into the Suva Shell depot to fill up his car, but workers locked him inside until riot police turned up to release him. The events sparked emergency government meetings, a media statement denouncing the workers for not using the proper channels of negotiation, and the Assistant Colonial Secretary authorised the breaking of the strike by any means necessary.

On the morning of 9 December, trucks fanned out across Suva to supply fuel to petrol stations under police escort. Anthony was at one petrol station when supplies arrived, and mobilised a crowd of 400 people in protest. At a second petrol station, a crowd of Fijian and Indian protesters gathered and formed a human barricade to stop queues of cars from driving up to the pump. Indian and Fijian drivers were persuaded to show solidarity by not refuelling. By the time the police arrived, only the European drivers remained. Staff abandoned a third petrol station and when a white Shell employee tried to take over operations, demonstrators sabotaged and shut down the pumps by removing the fuse box. The manager of a fourth petrol station fled when protesters arrived, telling the police that they could serve customers themselves. All throughout the city, bus drivers were confronted and the whole bus network was paralysed. Taxi drivers joined the strike, some abandoning their vehicles in the petrol queues or in the city with "on strike" scrawled across their windscreens.

Anthony requested permission to hold an assembly and address the crowds at a bus station, but the authorities' refusal didn't reach him. By 5pm, a crowd of 5,000 had materialised. One police officer's confused account summed up the mood:

> When we got there, the bus stand was absolutely full of people, women and children predominating. I think they were very excited indeed. I don't think they were alarmed. In fact, most of them seemed to be enjoying the situation immensely. There were crowds surging from one side to the other, singing nothing in particular – three cheers for this, that and the other... There were peals of very high pitched laughter. I did not know what to make of the whole thing.[21]

Another recounted: "The crowd was telling other people that this was their strike and inciting people to join in".[22]

The early attempts to disperse the crowd were met with boos, laughter and jeers. One person yelled: "The cops can do fuck all!" Police finally resorted to tear gas and baton charges into the crowd, who defended themselves by throwing rocks. The crowd scattered, swarmed the city and regrouped at various spots. A group of 100 men assembled barricades out of timber and steel drums. Over the next two hours, a riot broke out across Suva, with shops smashed and looted. Even after

---

21. Hempenstall & Rutherford 1984, p.80.
22. Hempenstall & Rutherford 1984, p.80.

the huge crowds dispersed, groups of Indian and Fijian youth engaged in overnight skirmishes with the police. The next morning, the military was called in, and police were given powers to arrest without warrants and impose a curfew.

On the afternoon of 10 December, the police granted permission for a mass public meeting in Prince Alfred Park, where it was rumoured that the strike leaders would be speaking. But when crowds arrived, they found themselves being addressed by three of the highest chiefs in Fiji, among them Ratu Kamisese Mara, the country's future first prime minister and later its president. They were joined by BD Lakshman, an Indian member of the Legislative Council. Together, the chiefs used their traditional authority to admonish and shame the crowd for their behaviour. The crowd dispersed peacefully and the riot ended.

Calm returned over the next two days as many Fijian workers began to return to work. Skeleton bus services began to operate and supply chains returned to normal, though the oil workers and taxi drivers remained on strike. But the mood was now subdued. In the meantime, the chiefs continued touring the city, holding mass meetings of up to 3,000 people where they argued that Fijians had brought shame to their villages, and implied that they had been duped by Indians. The Fijian president of the WRWGU was also impacted by these arguments. He encouraged Anthony to seek medical attention for exhaustion, then immediately called in Mara, who introduced union delegates to company representatives and negotiated a settlement on the company's terms. By the time Anthony returned, most of the union's executive had ratified the deal and he eventually relented.

The 1959 oil workers' strike is significant for a number of reasons. Firstly, it was the first urban multi-racial strike by Indian and Fijian workers in the country's history. Secondly, it demonstrated the potential economic power of the growing urban working class and its ability to rally mass support. For these two reasons, it terrified the colonial administration, the Indian bourgeois and the Fijian chiefs. The latter recognised that these developments posed a threat not only to the colonial state, but also threatened to undermine their own social position. They successfully appealed to indigenous Fijian identity to scuttle the strike, succeeding where the repressive power of the state and even the union officials themselves had failed to rein in militancy. In the aftermath of the strike, they funded and helped establish racially exclusive unions for Fijians in practically all industries, weakening the union movement as a whole. It illustrates the class divide that cuts through the Pacific and its various ethnic and racial groups.

The Bougainville mineworkers' strike of 1975

The people of Bougainville had a history of agitation against colonialism dating back to 1913, when New Guinea was still controlled by Germany. Welfare societies organised boycotts of taxes in the 1950s. In 1962 there was further resistance against taxation and calls for an end to Australian control over the island. The Bougainville national movement was cohering in the years leading up to the strike, as it became clear greater organisation would be needed to fight for the interests of locals against the mining companies.

After copper, gold and silver were discovered in Bougainville in 1964, the urban population of the island swelled from 750 in 1966 to over 14,000 by 1971.[23] Those who flocked there included people from other islands drawn to the opportunities of waged labour, and Australian expatriate workers who were required for the construction and operation of the infamous Panguna mine, which opened in 1969. The Australian labourers brought with them some of the militant traditions of the time, and in mid-1970 staged a strike which secured an agreement in line with other mining and construction agreements in Australia – including better wages, a closed shop, recognition of union delegates and on-site facilities for the union. For the Papua New Guinean workers employed by Bougainville Copper, who were still on $15 per week compared to the $200 per week minimum achieved in the new agreement, the Australian workers' win showed what unions could achieve.[24] In October 1970, the Bougainville Mining Workers' Union (BMWU) was established. It brought into its ranks Bougainvillean workers who had been part of nationalist and separatist movements.

The company consciously used the rationale of "relating Australians to Australian conditions, and locals to local conditions" to

23. Mamak & Ali 1979, p.72.
24. Hess, Maidment & Gima 2016, p.24

justify appalling disparities in pay between the two sections of workers. There were also significant disparities in the housing and facilities available to the two workforces and the company consciously sought to sow divisions and keep the two groups separate outside the workplace. One company foreman explained why mixed social events were once common but became rare: "We stopped these meetings some time ago when we found out that all it took was a few drinks before their underlying hostility towards us would surface".[25]

The union began with 51 members but by 1973 had over 800 members. The number of work hours lost due to strikes at Panguna rose from 230 in 1972, to 500 in 1973, to over 60,000 in 1974.[26] This included a two-day strike of over 2,400 workers in June which won an 18.5 percent pay rise and concessions in accommodation. When the minimum wage was increased in October, a two-day strike of 1,500 workers demanded that the increase flow on to the lowest paid workers at the site. Yet despite the company's assurances, the increase hadn't been passed more than six months later.

The 1975 strike and riot involved over a thousand mineworkers. They included workers from Bougainville and those who had migrated from other parts of PNG in search of work. The dispute was sparked by the dismissal of a union delegate allegedly involved in a brawl. Hundreds of workers began to gather at a nearby market while the union met with the company. Over 800 had gathered when the company announced it would consider the pay claim another day. Angry at the delays, the workers, brandishing sticks and iron bars, marched to the company's offices. Police fired tear gas and dispersed the crowd.

Rioting resumed the next morning. Again police fired tear gas, and called in reinforcements including squads armed with semi-automatic rifles. In the ensuing street battles, workers began to overturn vehicles, push them off cliffs and into rivers, and even ran trucks into police lines. They commandeered two bulldozers with which they proceeded to rip up roads, destroy mining equipment and even demolish the local police station.

By that afternoon, a heavy police mobilisation flown in from around

---

25. Mamak & Ali 1979, p.83.
26. Hess, Maidment & Gima 2016, p.32.

the country was able to break up the protests, ultimately arresting over a thousand workers. But only a few days later, fearing a mass breakout, the authorities released more than 700 prisoners. In September, 800 workers at the site struck in support of Bougainville's declaration of independence. Finally, in November a tribunal granted the workers' demands. They won over a million dollars in backpay and six-monthly cost of living adjustments. The company ultimately relented after appeals by the Department of Labour that the deal would be crucial to maintaining peace.

Throughout the mid-1970s, the Australian Council of Trade Unions under Bob Hawke had taken an ongoing interest in the BMWU, with Hawke personally receiving reports on the state of the union.[27] They noted that the union's leadership and official structures were weak, disorganised and unsuited to negotiations. After the dispute, the ACTU put concerted effort into professionalising the union, training its officials and dispatching officials from Australia to assist in reforming the union. These efforts included establishing a more stable bureaucracy and training 72 shop stewards in "basic diplomacy" to restrain any militancy which might run foul of the government and get company officials off-side. The result was that in 1977–78, the number of hours lost to industrial action was eight and over the next decade, the mine was able to operate with minimum disruption.

The story of the Bougainville Mining Workers' Union is an example of how, even in the Pacific, the politics that workers carry into their struggles can help shape and push them forward. But it also shows that, just as in the rest of the world, the conservative and class-collaborationist approach of reformist trade union leaderships can also restrain struggles. Politics is decisive, and an approach that looks to the self-activity and militancy of workers at the point of production is essential for victory.

The episodes examined in this article prove that the politics of working-class militancy and solidarity are just as necessary in the Pacific as they are elsewhere, and their relevance is not just confined to the advanced capitalist West.

---

27. Hess, Maidment & Gima 2016, p.26.

Conclusion

There is no corner of the world that is untouched by capitalism, or untouched by class struggle. This tiny glimpse of a rich and militant history of workers' struggle across the Pacific should highlight that the poor and oppressed of the region are not helpless victims waiting to be saved by one self-interested imperialist power or another. Instead, they are fighters with social power of their own and comrades to those struggling for a world free from exploitation. For anti-capitalists in Australia, this history also reveals the role our own government has played historically in holding the workers of the region down. Regardless of how military build-ups in the Pacific are justified by politicians in Washington and Canberra, it is a basic act of solidarity with workers in the Pacific to oppose every imperialist power circling the region. Finally, the history of class struggle in the Pacific confirms Marxism as a set of politics that can make sense of the world and articulate a strategy for liberation. Across the Pacific, there is a working class which shares the same interest in a world without capitalism, the same potential power to bring the bosses to their knees, and we share with them the same struggle to make that world a reality.

References

Amarshi, Azeem, Kenneth Good and Rex Mortimer, *Development and Dependency: The political economy of Papua New Guinea,* Oxford University Press, Melbourne.

Close-Barry, Kirstie and Victoria Stead 2017, "Remembering Australia's Wars: Hangings of Papua New Guineans by Australian Soldiers in WWII Complicate Our National Narratives", *Australian Policy and History,* 13 November. https://aph.org.au/2017/11/remembering-australias-wars-hangings-of-papua-new-guineans-by-australian-soldiers-in-wwii-complicate-our-national-narratives/

Frazer, Ian 1990, "Solomon Islands Labour History and Maasina Rule", *Labour in the South Pacific* (ed. C Moore, J Leckie and D Munro), James Cook University.

Frazer, Ian 1992, "Trade Unions and the State in Solomon Islands", *New Zealand Journal of Industrial Relations,* 17 (1), pp.23–37. https://ojs.victoria.ac.nz/nzjir/article/view/3310/2928

Gillion, Kenneth L 1977, *The Fiji Indians: Challenge to European Dominance 1920–1946, ANU Press.* https://openresearch-repository.anu.edu.au/handle/1885/115196

Hempenstall, Peter and Noel Rutherford 1984, "Industrial Protest Case Study: The 1959 Fiji Strike", *Protest and Dissent in the Colonial Pacific,* University of the South Pacific, pp.73–86.

Hess, Michael and James Gissua, "Unions and Industrial Relations in Papua New Guinea", *New Zealand Journal of Industrial Relations,* 17 (1), pp.39–55. https://ojs.victoria.ac.nz/nzjir/article/view/3311

Hess, Michael, Ewan Maidment and Keimelo Gima 2016, "Establishing the Bougainville Mining Workers' Union, 1969–1976", *The Journal of Pacific History,* 51 (1), pp.21–42.

Hince, Kevin 1985, "The earliest origins and suppression of trade unionism in the Fiji Islands", *New Zealand Journal of Industrial Relations,* 10 (2), pp.93–101. https://ojs.victoria.ac.nz/nzjir/article/view/3386/3003

Mamak, Alexander and Ahmed Ali 1979, *Race, Class and Rebellion in the South Pacific,* George Allen & Unwin Australia.

Moore, Clive 2017, "Trade and Labour", in *Making Mala: Malaita in Solomon Islands 1870s–1930s,* ANU Press, pp.83–138. https://press.anu.edu.au//downloads/press/n2401/pdf/book.pdf

Moore, Clive 2022, "Building society and the nation", in *Honiara. Village-City of Solomon Islands,* ANU Press, pp.297–354. https://press-files.anu.edu.au/downloads/press/n9664/html/ch07.xhtml?referer=&page=16#

Nicole, Robert 2011, "The movement for federation and the Viti Kabani", in *Disturbing History: Resistance in Early Colonial Fiji,* University of Hawai'i Press, pp.70–97.

Otago Daily Times 1920, "Fiji Labour Troubles", 3 March, p.8. https://paperspast.natlib.govt.nz/newspapers/ODT19200303.2.74

Riseman, Noah 2010, "Australian [Mis]treatment of Indigenous Labour in World War II Papua and New Guinea", *Labour History,* 98, May, pp.163–82.

Tribune 1965, "Tear gas used on Solomon Is. demonstration", 2 June, p.5. https://trove.nla.gov.au/newspaper/article/236347928

Sutherland, William 1992, *Beyond the Politics of Race: An alternative history of Fiji to 1992,* Australian National University. https://openresearch-repository.anu.edu.au/bitstream/1885/133703/4/Beyond_the_Politics_of_Race.pdf

Thompson, Roger C 1980, *Australian Imperialism in the Pacific: The Expansionist Era 1820–1920,* Melbourne University Press.

DARREN ROSO

Engels after Marx:
A (critical) defence

Darren Roso has published in *Overland,*
Revueperiode, Contretemps and *VientoSur.*
His forthcoming books, *Daniel Bensaïd:*
From the Actuality of Revolution to the
Melancholic Wager and *Karl Korsch: Heretical*
Marxist of Weimar Germany, are to be
published by Brill Historical Materialism.

In other words, classical Marxism should be submitted to
the same rigorous scrutiny and critical appraisal as the
post-classical tradition that derived from it. The courage and
calm needed for such a programme would be much greater
than in the case of Western Marxism, given the veneration with
which nearly all serious socialists have treated the classical
masters of historical materialism, and the absence to date of
any intellectual critique of these that remained equally and
resolutely revolutionary in political position. The greatest respect
is, however, compatible with the greatest lucidity. The study
of classical Marxism today needs a combination of scholarly
knowledge and sceptical honesty that it has not yet received.
– Perry Anderson[1]

I N NOVEMBER 1890, about seven years after Marx's death, Engels
turned seventy. Workers from the international socialist movement
around the world sent their gifts and messages in great number.[2]
Engels was physically thriving, remaining theoretically creative and
politically discerning; he was the most precious revolutionary – without

1. Anderson 1979, pp.112–3.
2. See Kapp 2018, pp.587–626.

equal – in the European socialist movement. Two of Engels' responses to his comrades, to Vaillant and the French Party, stand out:

> Destiny has willed it that I, in my capacity of survivor, should reap the honours due to the labours of my deceased contemporaries, and above all to those of Marx. Believe me, I do not cherish any illusions on that score nor on the very small part of all these tributes which is owed to me personally.[3]

And:

> You may rest assured that what remains to me of life and strength shall be devoted to the fight for the proletarian cause. When I am no longer capable of fighting, may it be granted that I die.[4]

With grace and humility, Engels had assumed many a great labour after Marx died. This work is of inestimable value. And without the protracted efforts of the late Engels, Marxism at the opening of the twentieth century would not have been what it became, in its Kautskyan Second International form. The task of this article is to explore that "minor part" Engels played without any illusion about the immense difficulty of the role and with the full view that Engels' life after Marx remained devoted to fighting for proletarian liberation.

The article explores three elements of the Marxism after Marx represented by Engels.

The first section analyses Engels' *political thought* after Marx's death, much of which comprises new introductions and rectifications to the classic texts he and/or Marx had written some time earlier, supplemented by an extensive correspondence. Political thinking is at the crux of these efforts as Engels searched for a *new revolutionary tactic* in the 1890s while defending the use of universal(ising) suffrage. Engels' political rectifications concerned tactics, not a transformation of strategy as a whole; the tactics sought were explicitly revolutionary

---

3.   Quoted in Kapp 2018, p.591.
4.   Quoted in Kapp 2018, p.592.

in character. Engels' political thought was a means to illuminate the unique possibilities of the situation he confronted.

The second part brings Engels' thought on history into view, partly to show how his approach ran counter to dogmatic ideological narrations of history, while also illuminating the primacy of politics in his turns to history, specifically drawing out his evaluations of the French Revolution of 1848 and the Paris Commune.

The last section pays attention to Engels' construction of Marxism at the unambiguously theoretical level. This is the most complex part, especially because no direct line to politics exists between the unambiguously theoretical level and the political. And yet, to take the theoretical arguments seriously, analysing their validity and truths is a necessary exercise. Throughout, I will take up Engels' ideas about the new materialism, the materialist inquiry into history, the critique of politics and the critique of political economy. These were years in which, if it were not for Engels' extensive labours, the scientific breakthroughs he and Marx were party to would largely have been forgotten or maligned beyond recognition. With Engels fortune was at hand. He was as capable an editor as ever, able to clean up Marx's unfinished manuscripts, and defend, explain and extend Marxism into new domains of fresh thought.

Engels' search for a new revolutionary tactic

Engels believed that revolutionary politics was more complex than any basic formula could capture, requiring a unique mode of thinking that is not repetitive precisely because it concerns singular situations. He recognised that schemas of the past can obstruct understanding of the present that constitute such singularities of history. Since Engels was a subtle and sophisticated thinker aware of the conditions of possibility of revolutionary politics, his late years cannot be read as a final consummation of some kind of dogmatism. Indeed, if Engels' own independent and early writings like *Outlines of a Critique of Political Economy* and *The Condition of the Working Class in England* were everlasting contributions to the genesis of Marxism, based as they were on the complex consistencies of class struggles, it is still worthwhile reading Engels' thinking *backwards*, from its most mature form to youth. Only from the mature writings can we ascertain the decisive arguments that were closed and left open by Engels at the time of his death. Of great interest then is the fact that Engels arrived at the terminus of his life while still searching for a new revolutionary political tactic.

It is instructive to note that Engels' last decade, and his last five years particularly, were years in which he not only set a certain revolutionary political tone for those committed to European socialism, but he also made efforts to set the political record straight. This is the background to the *Introduction* he penned to Marx's *Class Struggles in France,* and in many respects, the Paris Commune – as both harbinger of proletarian rule, and problematic failure to overcome – was pinned onto the canvas of that background.[5] On a number of occasions, Engels clarified the centrality of the political rule of the working class, the dictatorship of the proletariat fundamental to his perspective, none of which was gradualist or reformist.[6]

Engels consistently refuted contemporary critics who thought he and Marx were economic determinists who saw no place for political struggle and political force in history. Engels retorted that if they were economic determinists, they would not care a jot for the political rule of the proletariat.

Undaunted, Engels caused outrage among the Social Democratic Party leadership and the parliamentary fraction when he released Marx's critique of Lassalleanism, the *Critique of the Gotha Programme.* The intervention exposed Marx's criticism of the 1875 program to the rank and file of the party. As Yvonne Kapp writes:

> The resurrection of this old but by no means outdated document did more than flutter the dovecotes; it put the cat among the pigeons, for it challenged not simply the Lassalleans of sixteen years before but every present organisation, in Britain as on the Continent, which professed itself Marxist and claimed to represent the ultimate interests of the working class.[7]

---

5.   See Engels 2010c, pp.506–27.
6.   For a résumé of Engels' positions I summarise here, see Draper 1977, pp.307–25.
7.   Kapp 2018, p.609.

And in the interests of political clarity through the visual, Engels then defended the Paris Commune (while introducing Marx's *Civil War in France*), pointing to it as an example of what the dictatorship of the proletariat actually was: the Paris Commune, workers in arms, taking over a city and becoming the dominant class, despite the fact that they were eventually defeated.

And lastly, Engels defended – in his criticisms and proposed corrections to the 1891 *Erfurt Programme* – the democratic republic, which he understood to have been the concentrated political power of the working class, in the sense of the dictatorship of the proletariat. At each of these non-exhaustive returns to the role of the working class, its efforts and prospects for political rule, Engels adopted a revolutionary line aligned to the self-emancipation of the working class.

Engels' *Political Testament,* his *Introduction* to Marx's *Class Struggles in France,* is among the most contested of his writings, because it raised the stakes about whether he was for or against the revolutionary-insurrectional overthrow of the reigning constitution in Germany, on what terms, and under what conditions. Engels posed the question in 1895, quite explicitly, in the last text he ever wrote.[8] It seems that Engels did not think of the document as his definitive political testament, though *de facto* it became as much. In these late years, Engels was the closest he had ever been to German Social Democracy and its sister organisations, he was most integrated into the political and organisational functions of Social Democracy, and his every word to defend, extend and rectify Marxism was widely used and misused. Engels was intimately connected to the different national sections of the European and non-European socialist movement through his letters, oral discussions, correspondence and advice, being somebody who could be relied upon to judge political events. Nevertheless, Engels was tasked with updating and thinking through Marxism in the novel conjuncture of the late nineteenth century. The Anti-Socialist Laws had lapsed, Social Democracy could operate legally and Engels thought that a new political situation had begun in Germany.

For the first time in Europe, a mass party with hundreds of

---

8.   For secondary material on Engels' *Political Testament* I draw on Krätke 2020.

thousands of members and voters was based on a program of "scientific socialism". Engels wrote the *Introduction* between February and March 1895. At the time, the Chancellor of the Reich had introduced an anti-subversion bill designed to curtail Social Democracy's room for manoeuvre, and the context partly explains why eventually three versions of Engels' text entered into circulation: Engels' original version, the edited version, and a version not authorised, but in fact protested against, by Engels himself.

With rival versions of Engels' *Introduction* in circulation, the document was clearly a site of political struggle. Engels overtly and critically reflected upon the implications that flowed from the transformations of the modern bourgeois nation-states in a phase of accelerating geopolitical rivalry and industrial development. The capitalist mode of production had consolidated its rule over most social formations of Europe, and the state machines were becoming, or had indeed already become, more "bourgeois" – centralised and rationally bureaucratic – by the hour. With the modernising military machines, the industrial transformations and the mass organisational and electoral growth of German Social Democracy, the conditions of class struggle had already changed in scale and scope compared to the 1848 revolutions. In these conditions, Engels defended a medium-term application of a parliamentary tactic oriented to universal suffrage.

Engels carried out a specific operation in the *Introduction*, setting a problem he left unresolved. His stated problem? How was it possible for Social Democracy to build up sufficient hegemony to overthrow the modern state and the domination of capitalist production? Four interrelated elements met in this problem: materialist method, illusion, historical transformation and the power of the modernising nation-state. These elements confronted Social Democracy with questions about its political orientation and direction. To answer Social Democracy's want of political orientation, Engels had seen the need to underline that in terms of *method*; there is a *structural disjuncture* built into his and Marx's materialist inquiry into history, which pertains to their politics. If, in the last instance, economic causality triumphs in shaping historical events, then there remains a lack of contemporaneity between a class analysis based upon past economic developments and the political situation of a singular present – in other words, a lack of identity between the singular situation confronted and the knowledge of the materially existing social relations of production of the concrete situation themselves. Engels thought, without any shadow of a doubt, that materialist inquiry into history's structural disjuncture is a source of *error* and *illusion* for political practice and that it was necessary to rectify the illusions produced by the ways in which the situation of the 1848 revolutions appeared to him and Marx. Partly, to do this, Engels self-reflectively underlined the way a materialist inquiry needs to be conscious of its limits and structural disjuncture, all the while acknowledging that Marx's political writings on the 1848 revolutions had withstood the test of time in their ability to grasp events. Historical transformations and the developing military machines sharpened the possibilities of illusion implicit in an application of the materialist method unconscious of the structural disjuncture, and at the very least, Engels was warding off a form of impatience that insists on blind alleys which, on his interpretation, would have meant a quick ruin of the revolutionary project.

Upon entering the continent-wide uprisings of 1848, Engels and Marx shared the illusions of their generation, consisting in the expectation that the course of the revolution would follow the line of development modelled on the Great French Revolution. Expected was a rerun of the classical form of bourgeois revolution, which as it turned out was also the rarest and most atypical of its forms. From this classical form, they then deduced the possibility of a permanent revolution leading to proletarian revolution. Of central significance was the possibility that the 1848 revolutions would pass over from the bourgeois revolution to a proletarian revolution, a transition from revolutions made by minorities – or in the interest of these minorities – to revolutions of the immense majorities in the interest of the majorities. The Parisian uprising of June 1848 signalled the transition, posing the new utopian possibility on the historical stage.

However, according to Engels, the transition – in certain fundamental respects – failed. And why did it fail? In short, the undeveloped material formation of the continental working classes was not yet conducive to the abolition of capitalist production. Actually, the reverse was true, since capitalist domination and development were only just beginning to accelerate and consolidate on the European continent (which leaves aside even the rapid bourgeois transformations of America). After the defeat of the 1848 revolutions, Napoleon III and Bismarck would preside over rapid industrialisation projects. The small size of the proletariat, despite its political influence throughout events, partly explained the missed transition from a bourgeois to a proletarian revolution. In that context, Engels also thought that with the defeat of the 1848 revolutions, the period of revolutions *from above* had begun anew, what came to be called "passive revolutions", marked by the provisional – though far from definitive – end of revolutions from below.

With these retrospective judgments, and at an elementary but by no means insignificant level, Engels, in his *Introduction* to Marx's *Class Struggles in France,* was engaged in a defensive political operation, meaning he was warning German Social Democrats (a warning and not a definitive last word) about what not to do in the present context and what to continue to do. Engels had his eye on the immediate to medium-term prospects of the European socialist movement that was rapidly gaining in moral, hegemonic, electoral and social strength. In this situation, it seemed imperative not to cede any ground to the bourgeois and other opponents of Social Democracy who were trying to draw the party onto the streets in an open confrontation that would make it easier for the military and state machine, and opponents of Social Democracy, to win a swift and conclusive victory against the growing Social Democratic strength. Engels deliberated upon the complex relationship between the long-term process of building the socialist movement in Germany and the revolutionary event, the rupture, the moment of confrontation that could shatter the modern bourgeois state machinery. However, he did in fact warn against, and wisely so, any form of ultra-left madness or trap set by an anti-socialist provocation that could have derailed the growth of German socialism.

Perhaps it is scandalous to some readers that throughout his text, Engels clearly argues that barricade fighting along the lines of 1848 – Paris, Berlin or Vienna-style – was a thing of the past, only to return, possibly sporadically, and most often to be defeated. For Engels, the only way such barricades, street fighting and insurrections could have any chance of victory against the military was if the civic guard stood in the way between barricaded workers and the youth on the streets, in opposition to the military. By contrast, a direct, sharp and open confrontation between the insurrection and the military itself would invariably lead to the collapse and defeat of the exposed revolutionaries. If this was the case in the 1848, then it became much more pertinent, and the challenges much greater, against the military machine of the modernising capitalist states, with the technological innovations of their instruments of oppression (much of which was being tested in brutal colonial campaigns), through to the organisation of strategy and tactics that they could deploy against street movements. This much Engels argued. But the crux of his argument was a recognition that with the renovation, extension and massification of the military machines of the competing nation-states, it was possible for the morale of the military to break down, especially if Social Democracy had patiently built up hegemony throughout society at large. With Social Democracy a mass party and conscription in place, this might also mean rank-and-file soldiers not firing on their party comrades.

The case for *hegemony* was at the core of Engels' defensive political operation. It would subsequently flow into many of the debates about strategy and tactics among Marxists in Western Europe, with their divergences over the complex articulations of long-term building and short-term confrontations. Even if Engels didn't use the terminology that became currency among Western socialists, his argument in favour of the long-term processes of politically building Social Democracy's strength was a matter of hegemony: hegemony among the working class and layers of the middle classes and the peasantries rallying behind a socialist call led by the working class. Although the key weapon at the time was the use of universal(ising) suffrage through propaganda and the contestation of every representational post of Germany, Engels nevertheless accepted the need to confront the right wing of the Social Democratic Reichstag fraction when necessary. Though Engels formulated German socialism's road to influence in the problematic terms of a certain and tranquil march, he nevertheless was defending the need to use every *legal avenue* for socialist growth while not disavowing or forcing the use of *illegal methods of organisation,* party work and class struggle; if socialist politics could exploit legality, then so be it until the situation shifted, making other means necessary. That is how Engels seemed to have reasoned.

In form and essence, Engels' *Introduction* was edited to take the bite out of it by Wilhelm Liebknecht, who in *Vorwärts* presented Engels as a peace-loving gradualist smitten with legality. Notwithstanding the edits, Engels presented a very clear argument for revolutionary confrontation, not only by making the case for a hard fought for hegemony prior to a decisive showdown with the state machine, but also when he pointed to the relationship socialists had to the so-called *political contract* of the modernised bourgeois states. Modern bourgeois states were the results of revolutionary transformations from below and above. By pointing to the political contract, Engels in fact hinted at the conditions in which effective rebellion, insurrection and a right to revolution would be exercised on behalf of the socialists. Contract theory has a history in bourgeois political thinking and while these bourgeois thinkers held that the contract between the people and the sovereign should be respected, the moment the political contract was to break down – many bourgeois thinkers like Hobbes were all too aware of the possibilities of it doing so owing to their immediate experiences of civil wars – then the question becomes a fight for absolute power and sovereign authority, in which resistance, rebellion and revolution become legitimate. Certainly, Engels was giving a *hint* about the conditions for insurrectional struggle – the broken contract. Once the contract is broken, then the absoluteness of power becomes pivotal, and for Engels, this could mean nothing more than the political domination of the immense majority of self-emancipating workers, which, in the context of the Germany of the time meant winning over a decisive section of the military, breaking down the hierarchies of the military machines, while also entering into a phase through which the socialist movement no longer ran through the legal growth of the socialist movement *as such* but opened up a whole new phase of class struggle with a revolutionary dimension.

Now, Engels' late intervention is a transitional text marked by evident absences. Transitional, insofar as the ongoing nineteenth century fusion of the state and nation was still unfinished, imperial rivalry was leading – as Engels himself predicted – to a new world war of a kind never seen before; the formation of the continental working class was creating the possibilities for new forms of class struggle like the mass strike and workers' councils. Engels' transitional political intervention stood at the borderline between use of the tactic of universal suffrage and the emergence of the new weapon of the mass strike in Eastern and Western Europe. As a transitional document, its absences must be acknowledged: absent is an attention to mass strikes, workers' councils and a coherent account of the structural nature of reformism – all being phenomena that emerged within a decade or so after Engels' death. Identifying these absences is more useful than any slips of the pen or defensive manoeuvres that had their origins in the non-revolutionary situation or censorship because they allow us to judge the development of revolutionary politics in East and West in the Second International.

Engels and history

With the structural disjuncture between materialist method and contemporary class struggles outlined above, I think that Engels approached history in a twofold way: at once as a materialist inquiry into history and a politically overdetermined device for orientation in the present. The materialist inquiry into history pertains to the *past* while the politically overdetermined device has its gaze on the *present* with a hope to shape the *future*.

To show another perspective on the same issue, two thoughts organise Engels' many returns to history. First, as an anti-dogmatic inquirer into past history, Engels self-consciously broke with ideological-philosophical representations of history owing to the materialist-scientific line of research which was able to bring into view the complex and plural developments of the history of pre-class and class societies. What is an ideological-philosophical representation of history? It is an *a priori* edifice of thought constructed to dictate where history will *end* (this is the teleological function of the edifice). Marx and Engels had polemicised against the ideological and *a priori* representation of history in their unpublished and unfinished *German*

Ideology manuscripts. The turn away from an *a priori* edifice of thought meant Engels was open to new historical discoveries that adjusted his theoretical conceptions. Engels was self-critical and updated his formulations in view of new scientific discoveries, pointing out and criticising the ideological conceptions that needed rectification or abandonment; thus, we see the practice of a continued effort of materialist clarification. Without Engels' open orientation, the thought of revolutionary politics dies. (In the sections focused on *metaphor*, I will demonstrate one way in which Engels handled the need for fresh thought and the tendency of inadequate schematic edifices to solidify into dogmatic constructions.)

In the second place, Engels invoked history in a political manner, meaning he observed history set within the already constituted constellations of the primacy of politics, in order to draw the salient lessons, identify the nodal points of transition to make sense of his present, to win arguments with his contemporaries and set out a guiding thread of politics in the new situations he faced, showing that Engels returns to history under the conditions of the political exigencies, purposes and needs of a present with the class struggle ordering its reference points.

i. Engels and "hitherto unknown" histories

One of the most significant post-Marxian corrections Engels made to the *Communist Manifesto* was the note (in the 1888 English edition of the pamphlet) to the classic formulation that the history of all hitherto existing society is a history of class struggle.[9] The rectification was made in light of the ethnological revolution in historical time, Engels' detailed reworking of Marx's *Ethnological Notebooks* and the American anthropologist Lewis Morgan's studies of the Iroquois and non-written history. In many ways, Engels' correction complements the other rectifications that he and Marx made about what is to be done with the state machine, because not only was the eternal presence of class struggle throughout most of history challenged, so too was that of the state (and women's oppression).

---

9.   Marx and Engels 2010, p.482.

Engels corrected the *Communist Manifesto's* thesis about class struggle with the recognition that non-written history could not necessarily be said to have comprised class struggles. Specifically, non-written history as a domain of research was quite unknown to Marx and Engels in 1847, or at least it was not put to use. That is to suggest that the vast majority of history *without* class struggle, state alienation and women's oppression was unknown to them. The transformation in this domain allowed the inner organisation of primitive communist society – demonstrated primarily but not exclusively by Morgan – to rise to the surface of "Western" knowledge, altering and confirming a materialist and scientific approach to history. About this passing of the unknown to the known, it is remarkable that Marx and Engels had made an argument about a communist society with its expansion of liberation, the abolition of class antagonisms and the state without yet having knowledge about pre-recorded history in their vast encyclopaedic historical knowledge. However, the knowledge of pre-recorded history opened a whole new terrain, an expansive field that was, in its own particular way, a kind of proof of the possibility of classless and liberated societies even if, in and of themselves, pre-class societies still were not the kinds of liberated societies Marx and Engels had hopes for in the future, and they never argued for a retreat to a "raw communism" without the liberation of the singular individual that had already been achieved (in its unfree property-owning manner) by bourgeois modernity.

Knowledge of pre-recorded history provided a materialistic basis to break apart the intimate connection (made by philosophers and teleological ideologists of history) that history had had to the pre-modern and modern bourgeois state apparatuses. For much of written history, history was what happened in and among competing states. But the fact that much of human history was without an alienated class state meant this ideological assumption could no longer hold. With the ethnological revolution in historical time and the break with histories written from the vantage point of states, pre-recorded historical excavation could begin to ask questions about the beginnings of human beings, their institutions and the times prior to state-class-gender domination, and specifically how they came to produce their forms of life. Materialist excavations of pre-recorded history were therefore epochal intellectual events because they showed that the pivotal historical transitions concerned not just the movement from traditional class societies (in "the West" from Ancient Greece, the Roman Empire or the Middle Ages) to modern bourgeois societies. Instead of this epochal transformation from pre-modern to modern bourgeois societies, alone deemed to be essential was the materialist discovery of traditional pre-class societies based on common appropriation and deliberation, showing the possibilities of societies without class, state and gender domination, and even societies that made efforts to consciously organise themselves with means to mitigate against the emergence of forms of domination itself.

Notably, prior to working over Morgan's research on the Iroquois and kinship, Engels gave us a glimpse into the materialist and dialectical nature of common ownership in his illustration of the "negation of the negation".[10] This is fascinating – though potentially misleading if the *limits of dialectical presentation* are not respected, because disrespect immediately leads to another teleological and ideological edifice. The example shows the interconnection of abstract theoretical argument and materialist discovery at work in Engels. Engels drew an abstract argument from Rousseau to show how initially a state of nature might be based on equality, then passes over to a stage of inequality (a negation of the original state), but which is then negated anew (negation of the negation) by the social contract that brings about a higher form of equality. This was an illustration of the way one might think history through dialectical transitions, from which Engels suggested: every so-called civilised people began with common ownership of the land, which became a fetter and was abolished, thereby instituting private property; after the institution of private property, a third moment emerges because private property has itself become a fetter. Crucially, for Engels, the third moment – the "negation of the negation" – does not lead to a restoration of the original common ownership but results in a more developed form of possession in common. These abstract ideas were made more complex

10. I draw from Engels 1987, pp.129–31.

by the materialist discoveries of pre-recorded history which henceforth became a fundamental element of conceptions of modern liberation, which were no longer returns to the *origin* but were sublated "negations of the negation".

Of great consequence, Engels' correction to the first line of the *Communist Manifesto* has the significance that it spelt the end of the *ideological* contestations about the state of nature, about whether humans were naturally competitive or sociable and peaceable, which of course were projections of modern bourgeois society onto the past – articulated at different moments, from Hobbes to Locke, of the rise of capital – for the purposes of unifying, consolidating and reproducing the self-image of bourgeois society in the context of colonial expansion and subjugation. The excavation of pre-recorded history ends this ideological conflict in the direction of a materialist solution. Engels took these discoveries and additionally, based on Darwin's theory of evolution, could set them to work in texts like *The Part Played by Labour in the Transition from Ape to Man.*

ii. Engels and the memory of the Paris Commune

Engels returned to the history of nineteenth century revolutionary upheaval on many occasions, and here I turn to the eternally heroic Paris Commune. It shows the way Engels approached history under the condition of the primacy of politics, the second feature that organises his return to history. Twenty years after the defeat of the Paris Commune, Engels wrote an introduction to Marx's *The Civil War in France,* with the express intention of defending the nature of workers' power, but also to show the ironic limitations of the Proudhonists and Blanquists. Engels returned to the Commune to draw out the lesson that the old state apparatus as it had been shaped in the aftermath of the French Revolution could not be simply taken over by the proletariat.[11] Crucially, Engels was concerned about the way Parisian workers, and the politicised proletariat generally, had been deprived of their arms at every pivotal juncture of bourgeois revolution prior to the Commune. Engels discerned a kind of law of counter-revolution, a first

---

11.　Engels 2010b, pp.179–91.

commandment of the bourgeoisie in times of revolutionary turmoil, in which arms in the hands of the workers had to be taken away for the stabilisation of bourgeois rule to take place.

Engels' politicised approach to history was indexed to the needs of working-class self-emancipation. In that sense, Engels' return to the Commune was about generalising the lessons of revolutionary class struggle, part of an effort to orient the emerging socialist movement by way of historical exemplification. The politically orienting nature of the text is most clearly demonstrated in his discussions of the Proudhonists and Blanquists active in the Commune. For Engels, these forces experienced the ironies of history. The Proudhonists, who were mostly opposed to forms of labour association because of Proudhon's dogmas, came out in favour of forms of workers' association and organisation. On the other hand, the Blanquists, who had been minority conspirators, had themselves turned into politicians doing mass work. And beyond that, while the Blanquists had been in favour of a strictly centralised dictatorship, in the context of the Commune – because the Commune represented a *non-State,* a state with the capacity to undo itself – they effectively put the call out for other Communes to be built elsewhere and for power to be decentralised. Engels also criticised the economic limitations of the Proudhonists and the Blanquists – the central error of having not seized the Bank of France to take charge of the wealth of whole sections of the French bourgeoisie, which Engels thought would have at least won better conditions for a peace between Paris and Versailles. The point of raising Engels' return to the Commune is to show that, while returns to history are informed by a materialist and scientific approach to history, the political judgments also matter, especially how they may act as memorial pointers for revolutionary politics about where things could go into the future, the two key points Engels drew being about the nature of workers' power and the limits of the Proudhonists and Blanquists.

Engels' theoretical-scientific-philosophical elaborations

Engels' later years were dedicated to the scientific-theoretical-philosophical elaboration of Marxism – though "Marxism" and "Marxist" tend to conceptually obscure the contents of Engels' elaboration, Marx and Engels themselves having used the terms pejoratively. We do not get very far with the claim that Engels simply built the foundations of Marxism for other Marxists, because we need – in the first place – to know what these might be. Engels was acutely aware of such an obfuscation, as is apparent from his letters.

Throughout this section on Engels' theoretical work, I will focus on four components: the nature of the new materialism Engels (and Marx) referred back to, the materialist inquiry into history as Engels tried to defend it in his letters (tentatively taking over and popularising the notion of "historical materialism"), the provisional, fragmentary and incomplete expression of the critique of politics, which I read as one of Marx's decisive yet incomplete breakthroughs, and lastly, the articulation of Marx's critique of political economy, primarily through the efforts to edit, translate and introduce Marx's *Capital* (all four so-called volumes). Without separating, identifying and grasping these four elements of Engels' scientific-theoretical-philosophical work (I have left out Engels' *Dialectics of Nature*) it is not possible to come to proper theoretical terms with the Marxism of the Second International.

i. Materialist anti-dogmatics

Exegetists of Engels have an obligation to think through, make sense of and explore his philosophical new materialism as it passes over to scientific practices. Such an orientation thinks about what Engels does as a materialist anti-dogmatic thinker.

Despite his continual philosophical reliance on Hegel's *Science of Logic,* Engels remained committed to what may be termed a new materialism, with which he carried out a specific materialist operation of thinking based on what he rationally derived from philosophy. The derivation of that which was of rational value seems to be a key to Engels' relation to the Hegelian dialectic. Engels' most far-reaching statement about the relation *Hegelian* dialectics has to *rational* dialectics concerned the fact that the two distinct, Hegelian and rational, modes of dialectic have the same relation as the caloric theory and the mechanical theory, and phlogistic theory to Lavoisier's chemistry. What is striking from Engels' own writings is that whenever he took up Hegel for his own purposes, ie, wielded some of Hegel's rational thought determinations for his own use, he had to disassemble Hegel and break Hegel's concepts out of the order they had in Hegel's system (because of its obsolete character) to draw something rational from them.

The new materialism conjoins two elements that need attention while also moving against a mode of dogmatic conformity in philosophy. The new in the *new materialism* points to the modernity of the materialism, a sublated novelty in relation to the antiquated materialisms of Democritus, Epicurus and Lucretius that had been challenged and overturned by the philosophical idealisms of Aristotle and Hegel, each of whom developed complex thought determinations in their oeuvres in ostensible opposition to materialism. For Engels, the mostly Hegelian thought determinations passed over into the new materialism, making it a sublated form of philosophy present in the background of his materialist scientific practice. It is of decisive significance, however, that Engels' new materialism was also informed by Darwin, or at least Darwin was integrated into Engels' reflections; in this sense, Engels was concerned about the nature of materialism *after* Darwin's discoveries (many philosophers, and even contemporary critics like Dühring, had failed to consider Darwin's significance for modern materialism) as well as Marx's own.

However, Engels was also intent on criticising contemporary philosophers and theoreticians who tried to "lay down the law" to the working class through some set of commandments; these somebodies were enunciators of what we could call the *idealist Master discourses,* and they were abhorred by Engels. This aspect of Engels' relation to philosophy has been overlooked, but I think it is one key to grasping his intentions, projects and accomplishments adequately. To grasp Engels' abhorrence of idealist Master discourses, it is perhaps gainful to draw attention to notions like the *conformity* to reason and elucidate the *mechanics* of an idealist Master discourse. The mechanics of conformity run as follows: the idealist Master discourse voices an eternal Truth, hoping their listeners or readers will be beholden to it, imprisoned by it, willing to act and think in conformity with it. One is then not permitted to deviate from the idealist Master discourse because to deviate from the enunciated norm is akin to deviating from reason and Truth; the idealist Master discourse itself closes the future off from its many possibilities of development. According to Engels, this orientation is *sectarian* in communist politics, which is why he spent much time loosening the grip of the idealist Master discourses that are incompatible with the new materialism. The idealist Master discourse is sectarian and incompatible with the new materialism because communism, which is a movement abolishing the present state of things, becomes falsely set up as a movement *compelled* to conform to an impersonal eternal Truth, which amounts to conformity to a God concept or to an impersonal concept that is exterior to history and the materiality of class struggles, but which has been voiced by a sectarian denying their finitude. The Truth becomes an entity outside of time and history and others are expected, or compelled, to kneel before it without discussion. At the time Engels was writing, his contemporary Eugen Dühring had set himself up as the personification of such an impersonal and eternal Truth, which is why Engels spent so much effort destroying Dühring's claims to omniscience and subjection to it. Engels' new materialism needs to be read in terms of its elemental break with Master discourses and obedience to their inevitable sectarian finitude.

The relations of Marxism and philosophy, and the political controversies associated with them, explain why Engels only publicly intervened to address philosophical questions when the conditions facing the European socialist movement required, giving his interventions a *reactive* character (fundamentally opposed to traditional systems of philosophy).[12] Engels' reactive relationship to contemporary philosophy is a well-established fact, flowing consistently from the materialist character of Engels' approach to class struggle, science and the dialectic. Engels shows us the snares any attempt to build philosophical systems in the socialist movement are likely to encounter. He worked to overcome the dominant bourgeois conception of philosophy, as part of his struggle against the illusion that philosophy was the locomotive of history. The early socialist movement had systems ready to hand, from the utopian socialists to

---

12. I draw on Labica's study of Engels here.

Proudhon and Eugen Dühring, who hoped in one way or another to produce proletarian systems of philosophy able to rival the bourgeoisie. Engels polemicised against this tendency and resisted the pressures of concocting a system. He did not definitively defeat the dominant bourgeois conception of philosophy (it returned in different guises in the Second International onwards) and he had certain illusions about it (he didn't adequately answer *why* philosophers built their systems), but generally he was quite clear about the stakes of his new practice of materialism.

Engels' understanding of the new materialism has a transition from *philosophy* to *scientific* practice built into it, which is open to debate, but without grasping this his work is liable to be misunderstood. If we take Marx as an example, it is obvious that he abandons philosophy and moves onto the terrain of the *critique of political economy*, the scientific production achieved by *Capital*; to restate this, *Capital* is not a work of philosophy and this is generally crucial for the application of its critique. In terms of my argument, at least three points become crucial for the sections below. First, one should think about what it means for Engels, or Marx, to have a theory of something in the strong scientific sense. Second, we need to resolve the confusion – prevalent among dogmatic Marxists – between ideological worldviews and the scientific search for truths that produce actual insight into reality, its laws, structures, tendencies and counter-tendencies. To resolve this confusion, one needs to cut out the form of dogmatics that treats any utterance of Marx and Engels *as part of theory*, of some Marxist worldview, whereby theory is degraded because it is incorrectly taken to encompass everything ever said by Marx and Engels. Failure to distinguish between scientific and ideological solutions to questions means positively opting for an ideological posing of problems that sacrifices their truth contents. Third, theory can be grasped with its own immanent guarantees of objective truth – internally – which are not simply reducible to the external history of practice against which they are verified; the latter sacrifices indispensable claims to truth in favour of pragmatism.

Engels never, or rarely, remains at the level of a philosophical materialism, and any commitment to a philosophical materialism is translated into a materialist scientific practice. By virtue of this Engels has at times been misread as having been a positivist, but it is instead better to read him as putting forward a specific form of materialist dialectic that made redundant a philosophy of history and nature independent from the moment of scientific application. Engels more or less explicitly states as much in his short pamphlet *Ludwig Feuerbach and the End of Classical German Philosophy* and his polemics against Dühring, where he rules out of court any conception of philosophy as a thought of the general totality that absorbs the specific materialities, discoveries, hypotheses and provisional conclusions of the sciences. Indeed, Engels recognised that a remnant of philosophy – logic – became an empirical science among others, and though he wasn't entirely aware of or on top of the new breakthroughs then underway in modern logic, he left open the possibility of new logical discoveries.[13] Nevertheless, this was a way of historically situating the passage from philosophy to science and the role of logic. Principally, Engels thought that philosophical efforts to put a claim on the entire system of things and their knowledge was not a specific task of the new materialism and the materialist dialectic. Besides, a consequence of effacing the distinction between philosophy and science is the illusion that it is possible to deduce a particular piece of concrete knowledge from general laws of dialectical thought, from philosophy (ie, from a higher form of ideology). There have historically been remarkable philosophical anticipations of scientific discoveries; however, creative and concrete knowledge is not produced by way of a set of three or four dialectical laws, nor from Hegel's philosophy of nature, or logic.

The content of the new materialism, as Engels defended it, also has a distinctive relationship to the radical bourgeois materialism of the English and the French. In his introduction to the English edition of *Socialism: Utopian and Scientific,* Engels had excavated his and Marx's polemics against the Young Hegelians from *The Holy Family.*[14] The intention was to demonstrate to the English contemporaries that materialism was part of their more radical past, but he also demarcated

---

13. Engels's reference to logic as an empirical science needs qualification – it is a *formal* science.
14. I draw from Engels 2010d.

the early radical bourgeois materialism from a materialism of *history* (a materialism cognisant of historical materialities) while also demonstrating the *Kantian impasse of agnosticism*.

This is decisive for a few reasons.

First, when *The Holy Family* was written, Marx and Engels had a materialism of bodies[15] but not yet a materialism of history (admittedly materialisms of history had already been developed by Vico, Montesquieu and Ferguson); where Engels demonstrates the contours of a historical materialism, it shows the line of division *against* the radical bourgeois materialists (for whom Engels had great respect). Moreover however, Engels showed that he was keyed into Hegel's thought determinations, specifically in his criticism of Kant, the "thing-in-itself" and agnosticism. Kant had argued that all we could know is the realm of appearances, beyond which there was a thing in-itself, a kind of God concept to which one might be faithful. Kant separated the appearance that was knowable from the unknowable thing in-itself, and Engels adopted – explicitly – a Hegelian line of argument against Kant by suggesting that all we can know is a conceptual space of arguments, discoveries, reasoning, judgments, inferences and material practices that make sense of the world, which makes the thing in-itself redundant. There is no need for an unknowable beyond of all this, and to claim as much cedes too much ground to the religious type. This matters for Engels' concept of the new materialism as I defend it here, since at no point did Engels ever defend a reductionist materialism. Instead, Engels defended materialism, excavated the English radical bourgeois materialism, then recognised the *historical* character of his materialism, and indeed accepted Hegel's argument against Kant's thing in-itself, which meant that the materialism Engels espoused was a materialism resting on the logical space of concepts and rationality implicit in humanly material practices. Engels grasped the new materialism in terms of the materialities of history and the logical space of rationality that systematic thought determinations bring together for truthful insight.

We need to inquire properly and creatively into Engels'

---

15.   See Wolf 2021.

conception of reason, which is something much more than an influence of materialism here and an influence of Hegelian thought there, but rather – as the polemic against Dühring indubitably demonstrates – is a novel way of articulating what can be meant by rationality itself. Such, at least, is the terrain upon which I think we can plod along Engels' proposals well.

ii. Constructing the materialist conception of history: metaphors, models and fetishism wedged between thought and practical application

Engels had the difficult task of warding off any efforts to block the way of inquiry into the complexities of history. Engels' task was simultaneously to show that the materialist inquiry into history was open to the complexities of plural forms of human life, was not a reductionist theory based on unilinear conceptions of history or a unilaterally determining moment, while also making every effort to name, capture and communicate a real scientific breakthrough for materialist history adjoined to Marx's name. With this difficulty in mind, I distinguish three levels of Engels' construal of the materialist inquiry into history.

The first level of construal concerns *thought* as Engels presented the thought implicit in the materialist inquiry into history, a means to *point* the direction of research into complexities (strictly opposed to a theory of general development).

The second level is that of *metaphor* taken in Goethe's sense – *Do not forbid me use of metaphor; I could not else express my thoughts at all.*

To express the thought present in the materialist inquiry into history, Engels had need of metaphor. Whatever the strengths of metaphor, it remains descriptive, able to describe the nature of a new thought, but because of its descriptive character, theoretical knowledge and practical application need to go beyond the level of metaphor.

The third level of Engels' communication of the materialist inquiry into history is that of *practical application* into the diverse domains of history, which in practice is not handled at the level of a general history or theory but in diverse and specific materialities. We have, therefore, *theoretical thought, metaphor* and *practical application*, each having a place in the communication of Marx's discoveries, discoveries that had a relationship to the pre-Marxian materialist inquirers into history (Appian, Montesquieu and Ferguson) and modernising historiographies of Engels' time.

Distinct from the *application* of the materialist inquiry into history, Engels tried to elucidate its nature and content in a series of letters to the younger generation of its practitioners in the Social Democratic camp. Engels' explanations were in letters, not to be taken as seriously as his other polished publications. He himself was clear about this. Yet, these letters have formed part of the debates over whether "historical materialism" was reductionist or not – the term appeared about the time of these letters, between about 1890 to 1892, in English and in German. The "historical" in historical materialism is to be taken as an adjective, not a substantive. Additionally, Engels' English term is simpler owing to the difficulties of translating the *"materialistische Geschichtsauffassung"* adequately into English. In fact, it seems that Engels took the term "historical materialism" from Franz Mehring's *The Lessing Legend,* in which an appendix dedicated to the term can be found, and Engels held it in high esteem.[16] We should recognise the fact that Engels was part of the genesis of the first version of so-called "historical materialism", with Werner Sombart, Mehring, Kautsky, Plekhanov, Labriola and even Bernstein playing their part, which cut against a rival bourgeois tradition in becoming – the German *"human sciences"* – with whom the early form of historical materialism was in explicit and implicit confrontation and dialogue.

Engels opposed turning his and Marx's materialist *inquiry* into a Hegelian *philosophy of history*. The singular cases of history had to be taken up afresh. This is neatly expressed in a letter he wrote to Conrad Schmidt (1890):

> In general, the word "materialistic" serves many of the younger writers in Germany as a mere phrase with which anything and everything is labelled without further study, that is, they stick on this label and then consider the question disposed of. But our conception of history is above all a guide to study, not a lever for construction after the manner of the Hegelian [*kein*

16. For a comprehensive overview of these issues see Küttler, Petrioli and Wolf 2004.

Hebel der Konstruktion à la Hegelianertum]. All history must be studied afresh.[17]

Generally, Engels relied on Hegel's thought determinations while drawing a line of demarcation against a Hegelian philosophical construction in the domain of history (which is consistent with his break with ideological representations of history). Beyond this immediate effort to draw a line between idealist constructions and materialist inquiries into history, and without questioning the validity and truths of the materialist inquiry into history as such, some of Engels's formulations, or his mode of demonstration, in his other letters can nevertheless be questioned.

I will discuss these in four steps: first, Engels' use of *metaphor*, then his reliance on natural *models*; I will take up the economic *fetishism* identified in Engels' letters, which became a point of difficulty for subsequent Marxists in the debates with the revisionists and, lastly, I will claim that there are no general laws of history. In other words, this section will go into the tensions and the limits of Engels' late clarifications, raised not to refute "historical materialism" *as such,* but to show that the moment of the emergence, elucidation and popularisation of a materialist inquiry into history that Engels was attempting to juggle was also bound up with a string of problems that need to be deliberated upon to draw out what Marx and Engels actually achieved in their theoretical-scientific-philosophical work, while also identifying the blockades, impositions and the blind alleys for materialist inquiries into histories. Cognisant of the fact that the single most important problem facing Engels' defence of Marx's scientific discoveries in the domain of history was the underdevelopment of modern historiography, and the difficult crossing from the *announcement* of a materialist conception of history to an *effected* scientific-materialist history, to pay attention to Engels' use of metaphor and the modalities of explanation from his letters may seem injudicious. However, I think Wolf is correct to suggest that since Engels' letters are interventions into an overdetermined historical conjuncture, they need to be read as historical

---

17.   Engels 1890.

documents in which Engels made every effort to oppose eclecticism in philosophy and the reduction of Marx's materialist inquiry into history to a sectarian dogmatic economism under the guise of Marxism – a tendency that was gaining ground in German Social Democracy.[18]

A historically situated reading of Engels' letters, and attention to his mode of explanation and argumentation, is justified in terms of the need for a theoretical reading of the confluence of truths and validity of Engels' arguments for their soundness, with the hope of demonstrating the provisional nature of his formulations, which Engels himself consistently repeats.

Two distortions of the materialist inquiry into history gained ground among the younger intellectuals of Social Democracy. Too much weight was given to the "economic factor" of history, and "historical materialism" was used as a phrase practically covering over their own lack of historical knowledge. Within the textures of Engels' interventions, he relied on metaphor. In itself, metaphor is not a problem, only becoming a problem if metaphors are taken to be sufficient for a systematic-scientific theorisation. Metaphor is an index of a lacking elaborated scientificity and Engels was entirely aware, it seems, of this lack, constantly warning his interlocutors of the provisional and incomplete explanations he gave. We can see that in the history of Marxism, metaphors have been confused with, or even have substituted for, systematised theoretical concepts.

Engels uses at least two genres of metaphor in his letter to Schmidt: *Newtonian* and *legalistic*.[19] In terms of the Newtonian, a double metaphoric model is at play, according with the Newtonian physics of his time (the dominant paradigm of scientificity), combining *optics* and *Newtonian mechanics*. In the first two paragraphs of Engels' letter to Schmidt, talk of inverted reflection owes much to optics – which was a forerunner of Newtonian physics and a dominant science practised by the likes of Descartes – and "inverted reflection" is conjoined to a model of *interaction* illustrated by Newtonian mechanics hoping to demonstrate the autonomy and reciprocal interaction of the constituents of a historical whole. That is why Engels writes that "Economic,

18. Wolf 2008, pp.140–56.
19. This is convincingly stressed by Wolf 2008.

political and other reflections are just like those in the human eye, they pass through a condensing lens and therefore appear upside down, standing on their heads" – an optical image used to clarify the relation the money markets and the state have to production via the division of labour in society. What is presented, therefore, is a *general picture* of historical materialism based on a double metaphor where Engels tries to make a case for the "unequal forces", in which the economic has the dominant weight over the political-superstructural ones.

The other – vertical – metaphor Engels uses is the "last instance" taken from legal vocabulary. The vertical metaphor of the last instance refers to the hierarchy of decisional entities from initial to last. It is the final court of appeal. This is important because with it, a legal metaphor is transposed onto a materialist and scientific account of history as a kind of last judgement. Yet, there is an implicit problem with the transposition of legal metaphors in this way because they tend towards absolutising isolated features of "historical materialism" – whatever is the last instance – or they tend to produce a false totalisation derived from the last instance decision. Absolutisation and false totalisation in this sense are inherent in the very notion of a sovereign decision able to decide on all possible objects, which informs the legal metaphor because they do not require any further justification. Wolf is probably right to claim that this legalistic metaphor comes into conflict with the other metaphors Engels used from optics and Newtonian mechanics, because in the terms of a vertical legal metaphor, the last instance sovereign decision is unlimited in its power and authority, once a decision is made, while the metaphors from optics and Newtonian are subject to the limited and given conditions in which they are applicable.

Three further lines of criticism and discussion can be directed at Engels' letters on historical materialism, namely those of Louis Althusser and Lucio Colletti, while Étienne Balibar's deconstruction of dogmatic forms of historical materialism is helpful too. Each author needs to be taken seriously.[20] These are criticisms that demonstrate the difficulties and the subsequent confusions produced by certain of Engels' formulations. For Colletti, a fetishisation of the "economy" could

---

20. My discussion draws from Colletti 1972, Balibar 1974 and Althusser 2005.

be discerned, while for Althusser, Engels' invocation of "individual wills" in history was an unnecessary philosophical regression, and for Balibar, there is no general theory of transition and history. Colletti's argument rested upon the insight that in Engels' explanations, the notion of the economy became, or was read as, a purely technical term to the detriment of its reference to social relations of production, ie, it was technical rather than social-relational. With this reduction, history is interpreted as "the epiphenomenon of technical change". In turn, this meant that certain Marxists – notably Plekhanov – thought they could reduce the complexities of history and the superstructure to a monistic principle, an economistic-technical object, the economy.

Althusser's case, in contrast to Colletti's, focuses on the way Engels (in his letter to Joseph Bloch) tries to explain historical events on the terrain of *individual wills,* which is a problem because on this point, Engels reverts back to a philosophical-legal-bourgeois ideological concept of *individual will* to explain history in contradistinction to a materialistic inquiry. The "individual will" had already featured in bourgeois accounts of history from Hobbes to Adam Smith and Bentham, but most notably featured in Hegel's philosophy of history as a key to the development of right and the modern bourgeois state. We need to see the difficulty at stake here, because in order to explain the materialist conception of history Engels needs to draw in an ideological concept that grounded bourgeois representations of history and he gets caught in a bind when he does so. Engels' bind returns us to the Newtonian metaphor, as Engels bases the role of individual wills on the Newtonian metaphor of the parallelograms of forces, ie, Engels is taking a proof from Newton and applying it to history via the bourgeois representation of individual will. What we get is a metaphor combined with the preeminent ideological presupposition of bourgeois political and economic thought, somehow to explain the materialist inquiry into history. These two criticisms by Colletti and Althusser might be swept aside as pedantic, but they nevertheless show the difficulty of trying to *metaphorically represent* Marx and Engels' signature scientific breakthroughs in the domain of history, between the thought content and practical application.

Of course, Engels was conscious that history was more complex than any formula could capture, and here, Balibar was correct to point out that no general laws of development, no general law of history and no general theory of transition exist. In this sense, it is questionable whether there is a general theory of modes of production. The general concepts (I am drawing on Balibar) that Marx uses – of the forces of production, the relations of production, the base and the superstructure, the articulations of the legal political and ideological elements of the superstructure as well as the concepts of correspondence and contradiction that form part of this nexus of concepts – only point us in a general or a formal sense when analysing the materialities of a complex historical content. These concepts cannot actually *anticipate* the content that will be discovered, and to ask more from the formal concepts of a theory is to fall into a supra-historical general theory that does not grasp the transformations of one mode of production to another. For Balibar (perhaps more important for the ambiguities and the absences within the metaphors of Engels' late writings on historical materialism) it cannot be said that there is a general law of historical transition or a general theory of historical transition, no theory of transition in general – taken in the strong sense of explaining the real causality of the process of transition – because every historical transition is materially and conceptually distinct and one is not reducible to the other.

I have raised these issues for the simple reason that no theory of history taken at the level of undue *generality* ought to be taken from a close reading of Engels' late writings. The corollary of this deconstruction is that a theological reference to history – invoked politically or theoretically – is ruled out of court as a servility to reified concepts obstructing the enlightened thoughts and practices emancipation requires.

iii. Developing the critique of politics: genesis and structure, general theory and form, specific concept of the state

To lay my cards on the table as clearly as possible, the premise informing this section is that the *critique of politics* is a real scientific object produced by Marx's epistemic breakthroughs. If this argument is correct, then it should be handled as such. As a real scientific object, the critique of politics concerns *first* the modern bourgeois state as a specific social form of impersonal power and domination regulating class struggles, *second* the new practice of politics informing revolutionary class struggle, and *third* the possible withering away of the modern bourgeois state with the abolition of class domination. It is not a claim about a fictional autonomy of the modern bourgeois state untethered from capitalist production, but points to the reconstruction of the inner structure of the modern bourgeois state in its "ideal average", which is to be achieved by taking the scientificity of its *form-determinations* seriously.

Engels was indeed aware of the revolutionisation of traditional political thought he and Marx had accomplished, which functions as the certainly insufficient groundwork for rediscovering the critique of politics. However, since Engels presented Marx's scientific discoveries as consisting in the theory of surplus value and the materialist conception of history, little was said about Marx's tentative and fragmented breakthrough for the *critique of politics,* which is in need of interpretation and systematisation. I think it is necessary for us to draw out Engels' relationship to the critique of politics, and I claim that both Marx and Engels paved the way for, and contributed to, the specificity of the critique of politics, which nevertheless remained an unfinished, unaccomplished project. Indubitably, I am not making an argument that politics is the centre around which history moves, nor that history rotates around the nation-state as such; such ideas were present in the contemporary socialist movement under the guise of the so-called theory of force offering a paltry alternative to Marx's and Engels' materialist inquiries into history. The theorists of force argued that politics (and state activities) was the determining factor of history. Such an idea, in part, rests upon the superstition of the state Engels had derided, displaced the state from the centre of history conceived of as the march of God on earth.

Two problems face the argument for the critique of politics as an autonomous object in Marx's work, half identified and elaborated by Engels. First of all, if Engels rightly rejected the theory of force, then does a critique of politics fall into its pitfalls? This can be ruled out of hand because the theory of force is a bad theory, unable to align to the critique of political economy or a materialist inquiry into history. Second, and more substantially, a critique of politics was not developed and systematised to the same extent, or at the same level, as the critique of political economy was. The second problem has often been explained away on the basis that Marx had hoped to write a book on the state in his initial plans for *Capital*, though this may be dubious because it subsumes the critique of politics into the critique of political economy, operating under the illusion that the modern bourgeois state can easily or unproblematically be *derived* from the commodity form and value, or assumes that the missing book on the state could have been filled in if one sticks to what became a (redundant) plan for *Capital* in any case. These two turns in argumentation fail to consider that the critique of political economy and the critique of politics are distinct objects, and that, while in need of articulation, the critique of politics needs to be developed in a critical confrontation with modernising political theory and historically existing bourgeois state apparatuses in order to begin to draw out, at the level of scientificity required, the structural mechanisms of the modern bourgeois state apparatus.[21] This in turn means that no valid reason stands in the way of an effort to accomplish for the critique of politics what Marx accomplished for the critique of political economy. A materialist history of political *theory* can be written if aligned to a systematised critique of politics that would ensure Marxist debates about the modern bourgeois state do not unconsciously return to, and pitifully re-enact, the lines of division and development within bourgeois political thought from Hobbes' *Leviathan*, Locke's political writings and Hegel's *Philosophy of Right* (to name only some).[22]

To reiterate what I am claiming in other terms, and to compound the problem, Engels' most canonical turn to the question of the state is a *historical development of pre-modern states*, empirically more or less true, most clearly put forward in *The Origins of Private Property*,

---

21. See the pathbreaking Balibar, Luporini and Tosel 1979 – especially Tosel's chapter.
22. My arguments are informed by discussions with Frieder Otto Wolf, especially his reflections on the impasses of the state derivation debates; I also draw from Wolf 2023 – an unpublished work titled *Finite Marxism*, forthcoming from Brill Historical Materialism.

the Family and the State. This is not a criticism of Engels as such; it is an effort to show the different ways of thinking about the modern bourgeois state. We need to see that the historical inquiry is not a substitute for a systematic theoretical articulation of the modern bourgeois state, just as Marx's narration at the end of *Capital* about the primitive accumulation of capital doesn't substitute for the systematic theory present in *Capital*. Importantly, this argument does not deny history, it is simply against the idea that a historical description of the state is sufficient for understanding the modern bourgeois state; the "really existing object" of the theory is the modern bourgeois state as it factually exists in history, recognising that the modern bourgeois state has arisen and will wither away in the time of history. But the point is that theory grasps and reconstructs the real mechanisms of the functioning and reproduction of the modern bourgeois state. Where history dives into the material of concrete singularities, theory *explains* how and why things are, and how and why things change.

The critique of politics as a perfected systematic and scientific theory of the "ideal average" of the modern bourgeois state remains absent *despite* the breakthrough Marx made towards a critique of politics. The absence has significant consequences. It means that the critical relationship to modernising bourgeois political theory was not made at the level of theory on a par with the way Marx carried through a scientific revolution against classical political economy. The arc of modern bourgeois political theory from Machiavelli and Hobbes, through to Kant, Fichte and Hegel, the liberal tradition and the Germanic *Allgemeine Staatslehre* involved a complex articulation of science and ideology in their efforts to grasp the structural mechanics of modernising bourgeois states – these different traditions have informed political thinking in the socialist movement from its right and left wings. Engels recognises the need to revolutionise these traditions, and did so – but without providing a systematised theoretical alternative, a fact that could be masked by the power of the critique of political economy and the materialist inquiry into history as well as Engels' descriptions of the pre-modern state.

We know that the state cracks our heads in the defence of capital, property and power but we should not let that very real fact allow us to lose our theoretical minds. The critique of politics has need of an articulated theory of the modern bourgeois state and arguments against such a need for theory could be equally mobilised against the need for a book like *Capital*. Of course, no direct deduction of concrete and situated politics can take place from a theory of the modern bourgeois state, just as no direct deduction of politics can be made from Marx's so-called theory of revolution. However, we need to be clear about theory to oppose the *immediate givenness* of the modern bourgeois state and its mystifications. With Engels, thinking about the modern bourgeois state had remained at a descriptive level; we need to move beyond description of the modern bourgeois state to systematically construct a theory. At the most elementary level, this implies the distinction between proper names and the structures of the modern bourgeois state that are personified in those character masks with proper names. To remain at the level of description is to remain at the proper names – the character masks of the given immediacy of the state. Not only can this be misleading, it is not an approach Marx or Engels took seriously in theoretical terms.

At this juncture of my case, Antoine Artous is helpful because he makes a very convincing argument about the difference between Marx and Engels concerning the nature of the modern bourgeois state, or at least the ways in which they formulate the problem of the modern bourgeois states.[23] The difference can be drawn out from volume three of Marx's *Capital*, where he outlined the relationship that *sovereignty* and *dependence* have to pre-modern forms of economic exploitation. Marx's emphasis is on the notion of sovereignty and dependence insofar as they constitute a state that is form specific. Marx presents a *form specific* state, speaking to the diverse forms of the state, which in terms of theory relies on the primacy of logic over history. The primacy of logic over history means that a theory of the modern bourgeois state cannot be reduced to a *historical narration of its genesis,* nor a transhistorical entity that can be grasped through a general theory of the state, but instead requires an effort that leads towards a systematic-theoretical reconstruction of the modern bourgeois state in

---

23. Artous 1999, pp.236–43.

its "ideal average" as it pertains to the structures of modern bourgeois societies. By contrast, Engels develops in *The Origin of the Family, Private Property and the State* – notwithstanding the vast thought and historical material contained in it and the relations it had to Marx's own research – a general theory of the state (based on a historical-genetic account of the state). Marx's and Engels' formulations are not the same, and can even be taken to be two conflicting orientations towards the modern bourgeois state because Marx points towards a *form specific state* (for which a form determinate theory understood in the Aristotelian and Marxian sense is required) while Engels identifies a *general transhistorical state*.

I should indicate a complexity of theory here: if one recognises the primacy of logic in the form specific notion of the state as Marx defends it – and Artous draws it out – it cannot be said that the modern bourgeois form of the state has yet been successfully theoretically derived from the relations of capitalist production and reproduction. Why is this a problem? Because on the one hand, while it might be correct to point to the need for a logic specific to capitalist production, modern bourgeois societies and the modern bourgeois state based on capitalist exploitation, the state derivation debates themselves (most prominent in Germany) reached an impasse, where they might have proven that it is not possible to simply derive the modern state logically from the capitalist relation, the commodity or from *Capital*; they may even have fallen into *the very antinomies that plagued modern bourgeois political thought,* in its moments of ascendancy and consolidation in relation to the Dutch, English, American and French bourgeois revolutions *and* the revolutions from above. Marx himself had entertained ideas about historically and logically beginning with the French Revolution as the starting point, since the modernisation of the national-state produced by the French Revolution had global implications, from colonised Ireland through to the Iberian aristocracies, Poland in the East, and Prussia (it is not clear whether Marx held onto this starting point or would have changed it).[24] As a consequence, while it might be necessary to produce a systematic theory of the modern bourgeois state

---

24. Teeple 1984, p.166.

(and its relation to international relations and gendered realities) based on the inner organisation of modern bourgeois societies in which the capitalist mode of production dominates, it may not be possible – this was proven negatively by the state derivation debates – to conceptually derive it from the commodity as such, the concept of *right* or the capital relation and may somehow run through an immanent critique of political theory-philosophy as it historically emerged and developed. One could write a history of theory for the critique of politics the likes of which Marx didn't complete even for the critique of political economy and the historical existence of the modern bourgeois state.

We need however to go beyond the logical and historical couplet that has animated these debates because it might be much more useful – when reading Engels – to understand the nature of a systematic theory building *as such,* and the relation it has to arguments made specifically on an empirical and historical terrain. Such a move overcomes the historical and logical couplet by showing the way systematic theory mobilises empirical and the historical arguments that cannot be contained in theory. We have a clear reference in Marx and Engels to do this, namely that of the self-conscious notion of the limits to dialectical presentation, which Marx and Engels seem to have thought was a fundamental feature of the materialist dialectic. When we think about a systematic theory articulating the structures of the modern bourgeois state, we are talking about a *theoretical-dialectical presentation.* And the limits of such a dialectical presentation can be made clear and exact, being those specific points where the systematic theory needs to refer back to its own materialist presuppositions and the contingent empirical historical facts a sequence of arguments might rest upon, which in principle cannot be entirely contained by any systematic-theoretical representation of the modern bourgeois state. I identify this because there seems to be a dualism between, on the one hand, an effort to conceptually derive the modern bourgeois state in an *a priori* sense, beginning with an elementary concept and working (along the Hegelian model) up to a finished form of the state in a theoretical representation; as opposed, on the other hand, to a historical account of the modern bourgeois state that essentially suffers from empiricism and historicism, capitulating to the *given immediacy* of the modern bourgeois state apparatus and its forms of appearance which produces a description aided by proper names to the detriment of a theory articulating the structures that are personified by such proper names. The consequence of breaking this dualism? One is able to think through a critique of politics by articulating a theory cognisant of its limits (in relation to empirical research and the historical modern bourgeois state) while presenting the complex determinations animating the structural mechanics of the modern bourgeois state apparatus in its "ideal average". This implies a notion of scientificity that recognises the validity and truths of the scientific-theoretical argument as well as the inevitable blind spots in any theory of the modern bourgeois state.

At the same time, Engels was writing in a century when modern bourgeois nation-states were rapidly transforming, rationalising and extending their bureaucracies, while consolidating, universalising and reproducing their forms of domination. To a certain extent, the process underway put limits on any ability to produce and elaborate a systematised critique of politics able to grasp conceptually – in the "ideal average" – the modern bourgeois state apparatus. We have in the late Engels, therefore, an interaction of a materialist analysis of the emergence of the pre-modern state and a contemporary identification of the militarisation of the state, forms of passive revolution underway, the strategy and tactics of the workers' movement faced with the modernising states. As the above has demonstrated, Engels also has a *revolutionary* argument about strategy and tactics which was left unresolved, and faced with the state and the need to provide alternatives, the Paris Commune was the exemplar of a dictatorship of the proletariat, but it is limited. Engels was able to make an argument for workers' power, but lacking is a systematised theory of the modern bourgeois state, a developed critique of politics, able to grasp the structural mechanisms and modes of reproduction immanent to the historically specific modern bourgeois state.

Though the critique of politics was not theoretically systematised, insofar as Engels grasped the modern bourgeois state as a machine of domination – the machine metaphor suggests that its structural mechanics can be grasped – he contributed to the critique of politics.

Factually, Engels speaks of the state as a machine, not a condensation of class forces; it is a material apparatus of domination that ensures the subjugated classes remain oppressed. Engels did so against the backdrop of a contingent history, developing his arguments in a range of interventions concerning the housing question, the unification of Germany under Prussian domination, the new materials dedicated to the re-edition of his work on the German Reformation and the Peasant Wars. The new material contained in the text concerned the decline of feudalism and the emergence of nation-states, very valuable because Engels tried to grasp the relationship between the emergence of the modern bourgeois nation-state and the rise of capitalist relations in the context of the absent German bourgeois revolution. Moreover, Engels polemicised against the state socialists who supported Bismarck's unification of Germany and the "strong state". Many diverse threads about the modern bourgeois state interweave and knot together, producing a concrete historical appraisal of the modernising bourgeois state apparatus, showing that this is not an area of exploration and thought that Engels simply neglected.

In bringing this section to a close, it is best I state that I think Engels is part of the brilliant transitional phase of Marxist scientificity concerning the critique of the modern bourgeois state. But nevertheless, it remains a transitional phase. Concerning the modern bourgeois state, Engels had his finger on the breakthrough of Marx's critique of politics without giving it a finished form. One effect was that the question of the modern bourgeois state was posed for future generations of Marxists, at least after the first version of "historical materialism" of the Second International. Future Marxists could choose to remain at the level of the transitional theoretical-description, namely at the level in which description wins out over systematic theoretical construction, or they could move forward in the direction of provisionally completing the critique of politics by constructing the theory and applying it beyond its descriptive weaknesses.

The lack of a systematised critique of politics had deleterious penalties for Second International Marxism, in part because the early generation of socialist writers effectively had to apply a critique of politics without the existence of the theory; I am consciously oversimplifying because in political practice (among the revolutionary left) the break was indeed present, but it had not been made conscious theoretically. Often, they did so under the guise of the materialist conception of history, as can be seen in the debates over the national question. Many of the most significant works were materialist inquiries into the development of the capitalist mode of production and the state, the role of the state in the imperialist world economy, the returns to the nature of the bourgeois revolutions in relation to the proletarian, among which Franz Mehring's *Absolutism and Revolution in Germany* and Eduard Bernstein's *Cromwell and Communism: Socialism and Democracy in the Great English Revolution* count as exemplary works. While still a revolutionary under the tutelage of Engels, Bernstein tried to think through the role of Hobbes and Harrington and seventeenth century political philosophy. It was, however, not until Lenin recuperated and salvaged the critique of politics in *State and Revolution* – tentatively and not definitively – that Marxists provisionally began to move away from a critique of politics applied half-consciously under the guise of the materialist conception of history. Even Lenin, despite salvaging the critique of politics, produced only a textual convalescence of Marx's and Engels' own positions, without extending them theoretically as such. Lenin represented an opening of a new terrain; however, before this new terrain could be productively tilled, since it was killed off quickly by Stalinism, the lack of clarity about the critique of politics flowed back into a lack of clarity about the relation socialist politics and class struggles had to the modern and modernising bourgeois state apparatuses in the East and West. In a sense, this key theoretical-political weakness of the Second International has yet to find its accomplished resolution – on the terrain of theory or the liberated fields opened by the withering away of the state.

iv. Engels and the critique of political economy
I finally deal here with Engels' editing, publication, interpretation and popularisation of Marx's critique of political economy and his rebuttal of contemporary criticisms.

Engels recognised with the utmost clarity, in ways that often have not been properly interpreted, the extent of the scientific revolution that Marx made in relation to the classical political economists who went before him. In the various forewords to the English and German editions of *Capital* volume one, and the prefaces to volume two of *Capital*, Engels outlines the structure of the scientific revolution Marx made for the critique of political economy. This is a decisive element of being able to recognise the contribution of Engels' interpretation of *Capital*. In addition, the fact that the question of abstractions and value became an object of debate and contestation immediately after Engels' death shows that conceptuality was at issue, which refers back to what has been dubbed the historical-logical approach to *Capital* – though Engels did not use the term, he influenced the interpretation.

The relationship between history and logic are at stake again in the debates about Engels' interpretation of the critique of political economy (though the debate over history and logic in *Capital* does not exhaust the reading of it). Again, the interpretation implies adopting a position on the nature of conceptuality – of the systematic-scientific discourse produced by Marx – which is a vital point of contestation in debates about Engels. For example, in the third volume of *Capital*, and in some of his letters, such as his correspondence with Sombart, Engels had expressed ideas about the historical emergence of value and the nature of concepts. Specifically concerning value, Engels posed the existence of the value form prior to the capitalist mode of production, which tended to obscure the historically specific nature of the value form, positing instead a transhistorical notion of value. Thus, in his redacted version of volume three, Engels wrote:

> In a word: the Marxian law of value holds generally, as far as economic laws are valid at all, for the whole period of simple commodity production, that is, up to the time when the latter suffers a modification through the appearance of the capitalist form of production. Thus the Marxian law of value has general economic validity for a period lasting from the beginning of exchange, which transforms products into commodities, down to the 15th century of the present era. But the exchange of commodities dates from a time before all written history, which in Egypt goes back to at least 2500 BC, and perhaps 5000 BC, and in

Babylon to 4000 BC, perhaps 6000 BC; thus the law of value has prevailed during a period of from five to seven thousand years.[25]

Engels' chain of reasoning runs as follows: when goods are exchanged there are commodities, if there are commodities then value exists, and when value exists the law of value is valid. Therefore, because goods have been exchanged for thousands of years, the law of value has existed for thousands of years. Engels' statement *might* be contextualised in the history of *commercial capitalism* that Banaji has gone to great lengths to establish, implicitly raising the status of value-relations prior to the domination of capitalist production proper.[26] Yet, even if this contextualisation is granted, it is temporally much more limited than the five to seven thousand years Engels refers to, and the suggestion that the law of value was valid before the rise of the capitalist mode of production of the fifteenth century still has the theoretical effect of turning value into a transhistorical object. Still, the contextualisation completely fails if Marx is correct to have claimed an elemental distinction between pre-capitalist commercial capital and capitalist commercial capital. And, Engels' chain of reasoning fails to do justice to the systematic-theoretical structure of *Capital*, since among other things it makes Marx's dialectical presentation in chapters like *Exchange* (chapter two) read like a *historical narration* instead of form-determinate moments of a theoretical argument concerned alone with the historical specificity of the capitalist mode of production.

Why does this matter? An interpretation of theoretical concepts in the critique of political economy and the systematic character of Marx's *Capital* cannot be sidelined, because a materialist reading of its scientific argument might be a precondition not only for a defence of *Capital* but the application of it in the research into contemporary constellations of capital. This is helped by grasping the relation the form-determinate systematic theory of *Capital* has to the historical. There is a backstory to Engels' interpretive error that runs to Engels' review of Marx's *A Contribution to the Critique of Political Economy* (1859). In this review, Engels had pursued a thesis about the method that

25. Engels 2010a, p.887.
26. Banaji 2020.

informed Marx's critique of political economy. The thesis stipulated that *logic* and *history* run in parallel development. This thesis gave rise to the logical-historical interpretation of *Capital* that assumed Marx's categories developed parallel to history.[27] Not only was this at odds with Marx's own methodological self-reflections (in the *Introduction* to the *Grundrisse*) that differentiated logical development and historical development in a way that did not allow for Engels' postulated parallel course, the error negatively influenced debates about *Capital* because instead of focusing on the limits to dialectical presentation, a kind of pseudo-problem was established that took attention away from the specific modality of Marx's systematic-theory building and the function his historical analyses and historical presuppositions had within it. Symptomatic of Engels' misinterpretation was the fact that Marx did not cite this text anywhere in *Capital*, not even in his post-face to the second edition of *Capital* where Marx clarified his materialist mode of dialectical presentation (Marx often cited Engels' work throughout the book).

Of course, the above is not to neglect the fact that Marx's work process was open and unfinished. It is unclear if Marx ever settled on a final *theoretical representation* of the critique of political economy. We have an openness in which history and logic tend at certain moments to intersect or flow in the directions of systematic scientificity or historical detail. The key example of this is Marx's editing of the French edition of *Capital*, which he had filled out in empirical detail and had gained in scientific rigour as a result.

The prevailing problem of the late Engels' relation to *Capital* has concerned his editing and publication of volume three of *Capital* and to a lesser extent, his plan to have Marx's volume four of *Capital* – the so-called history of theory – published as *Theories of Surplus-Value* (a plan executed by Kautsky).[28] Marx had advanced his preparation of volume two much further and it required less work (he wrote a completely new draft of volume two in 1870 and changed

---

27. I draw on Michael Heinrich's unpublished *Engels wieder gelesen: Seine Rezension von Marx' "Zur Kritik der politischen Ökonomie"*. I am grateful to him for it and for answers to my questions.
28. Engels 2010e, p.503. Heinrich had renewed the debate about Engels in Heinrich 1996.

it substantially in 1877). While coming to terms with the dispute, it is necessary, on the one hand, to keep in mind that nobody was ever or probably will ever be better placed than Engels to have handled Marx's unfinished manuscripts. If there is indeed a difference between Marx's original manuscripts and Engels' redacted, edited, arranged, finished and polished volumes of *Capital*, then this is by no means an easy question to answer because even if we were to identify the important points of divergence, the question would always arise as to *who* – in terms of the author of posterity writing – actually has more intellectual authority and depth than Engels did. However, this is not the decisive issue either, because the open-ended nature of Marx's project and Engels' interventions into it means one is not handling a *hermeneutic* problem to decipher the meaning of Marx's text but a systematic scientific critique of the structural mechanisms of capital that might be applied to the contemporary world. At stake are the scientific truths that Marx's critique of political economy produced and how they relate to the transformations of capitalist production in history. On the other hand, we now have Marx's original manuscripts and there is no reason why these cannot be the focal point for debates about the third volume of *Capital*; it is possible to see where Engels made his interpretations and editorial interventions. To capture this relation, falsification is the wrong word, especially because volumes two and three of *Capital* were less developed by Marx's own hand. Marx had mostly refined various editions of volume one, and between drafting volume three (the *Manuscript of 1864–65* that he returned to in 1868 and 1875) and his death, Marx spent about fifteen years researching new developments, captured in his 1870s economic writings – it matters not only how Engels might have edited things, but the distance crossed between the draft of volume three and the new research Marx actually delved into and any discoveries he made.[29]

Somewhat distinct from the debate over falsification, too little attention is paid to what is in fact a key issue – the way Engels grasped the history of natural sciences and their scientific revolutions and conjoined this understanding to his exposition of Marx's critique

---

29. Moseley 2018, pp.121–4.

of political economy. In fact, Engels unequivocally recognised the scientific revolution, and even gave a working concept of a scientific revolution and how to read the effects of it, initiated by Marx's *Capital* – all three volumes constituting the revolution. The concept of Marx's scientific revolution was most explicit in Engels' preface to the second volume of *Capital*, in which we discern not only a concern for Marx's discoveries, but also Engels' painstaking work concerning the history of the sciences. Engels was, it needs to be said, singularly placed to articulate Marx's mode of scientificity and this is a matter of theoretical consequence. An understanding of Marx's relation to the classical political economists, and the structure of his scientific discovery, needs to begin with Engels' thoughtfulness. Simply put, the second volume of *Capital* and Engels' interpretation of it is of significance precisely because Engels was already thinking about and was extremely well versed in the history of the sciences and the history of the scientific revolutions. Thus, Engels was well able identify the character of Marx's scientific revolution against classical political economy. Engels' insights can shape the way in which we think about Marx's achievements. This is a feature of Engels' work after Marx that needs the full recognition it deserves. Indeed, Engels also contributes – in the domain of classical political economy and critique of political economy – to an understanding about the nature of scientific revolutions as such, by practising the continuation of it – which means that these revolutionary scientific works also probably contained implicit errors that need to be addressed explicitly (this is the only position congruent with the strong claim for a scientific breakthrough).

On a final note, regarding the critique of political economy, Engels had made every effort to come to terms with the transformations of the modern capitalist mode of production. This was an unfinished effort, requiring the application of Marx's critique of political economy to new concrete situations. We see Engels address the transformations of the capitalist mode of production in the preface to the English edition of *Capital* and his *Supplement to Capital, Volume Three* concerning the stock exchange and colonialism. Jairus Banaji has captured what this meant for the development of the new epoch of imperialism (and theorisations of it):

As Engels drew closer to the end of his life in the 1890s...oil, steel, and chemicals, not textiles, became the typical face of large-scale industry. In his addenda to volume three of *Capital*, Engels' sense of this new capitalist modernity was reflected in belated references to the surge of competition between "a whole series of competing industrial countries" and to "gigantic" concentrations of capital in "cartels" and "trusts". All this was new, anticipated but never witnessed by Marx. But the sense of capitalist novelty was of course also reflected in admiring references to the way submarine telegraph cables, steamers, and the completion of the Suez Canal had all dramatically compressed or accelerated the turnover of world trade. Between the writing of *Capital* and Engels' additions to the text a completely new world had emerged, defined by a much sharper sense of nationality, greater aggression in world politics, and a sense of living at new velocities.[30]

Engels' hints and insights were further developed by the subsequent debates in the Second International from the 1890s onwards concerning the reform and revolution debates and the development of an imperialist world economy. In this sense, Bernstein (who overestimated new developments of capitalist concentration, reading them as an amelioration of tendencies towards crisis), Kautsky (who built a historicist orthodoxy through his popularisation of Marx's *Capital* but produced excellent studies of the agrarian question), Luxemburg (who had a uniquely critical relationship to Marx's *Capital* and was not afraid to criticise the old Moor in view of new truths), Hilferding (who misunderstood the role of critique but articulated the high powers of banks and joint-stock companies and the extent to which they shaped social, political and international life), Lenin (who remained descriptive and hardly produced a theory but nevertheless tried), Bukharin (perhaps the strongest writer capturing global imperialism at the intersection of the state and capital), were all figures locked into a debate, constituting a further scientific continuation of searching points that Engels left hanging at the point of his death, but which

30. Banaji 2020, p.122.

were pivotal in the application of the critique of political economy to a transforming world that was to create the conditions for revolutionary transformations in Russia and possibly also in the West.

A late Engels for our times

We ought to return to Engels' letter to the French Party written on his seventieth birthday. Engels' life and strength were dedicated to fighting for the proletarian cause, the most imaginative, comprehensive and insubordinate cause of our modernity, if only we lend an ear to it and listen to its voice. Without Engels' determination to fight, the historically specific Marxism he helped forge would not have been. It is our task today to fight in the spirit that Engels has left to those of his present survivors well over a hundred years after his departure. But it is also our task to think the theoretical while fighting through the political, without presumption or pretension. It is the task of a new, youthful generation of revolutionary Marxists – inclusive of those to be – to overcome the limits, blind spots and aporias of the historically revolved and ended Marxism that Engels had helped to build so we may think of the variants and invariants of the world Engels shared with us, fighting for the proletarian cause.

References

Althusser, Louis 2005, "Appendix", in *For Marx*, pp.117–28, London: Verso.

Anderson, Perry 1979, *Considerations on Western Marxism*, London: Verso.

Artous, Antoine 1999, *Marx, l'État et la politique*, Paris: Syllepse.

Balibar, Étienne 1974, "Sur la dialectique historique", in *Cinq Études du matérialisme historique*, ed. Louis Althusser, pp.205–45, Paris: F. Maspero.

Balibar, Étienne, Cesare Luporini and André Tosel 1979, *Marx et sa critique de la politique*, Paris: F. Maspero.

Banaji, Jairus 2020, *A Brief History of Commercial Capitalism*, Chicago: Haymarket Books.

Colletti, Lucio 1972, "Bernstein and the Marxism of the Second International", in *From Rousseau to Lenin: Studies in Ideology and Society*, pp.45–108, London: New Left Books.

Draper, Hal 1977, *Karl Marx's Theory of Revolution III. The "Dictatorship of the Proletariat"*, New York: Monthly Review Press.

Engels, Frederick 1987, "Anti-Dühring", in *Marx Engels Collected Works*, Moscow: Progress Publishers.

Engels, Frederick 2010a, "Engels, Supplement to Capital, Volume Three", in *Marx & Engels Collected Works*, pp.875–97, Digital Editions: Lawrence & Wishart.

Engels, Frederick 2010b, "Introduction to Karl Marx's *Civil War in France*", in *Marx & Engels Collected Works*, pp.179–91, Digital Editions: Lawrence & Wishart.

Engels, Frederick 2010c, "Introduction to the *Class Struggles in France*", in *Marx & Engels Collected Works*, pp.506–24, Digital Editions: Lawrence & Wishart.

Engels, Frederick 2010d, "Introduction to the English Edition (1892) of *Socialism: Utopian and Scientific*", in *Marx & Engels Collected Works*, pp.278–302, Digital Editions: Lawrence & Wishart.

Engels, Frederick 2010e, "On the Fourth Volume of Karl Marx's *Capital*", in *Marx & Engels Collected Works*, p.503, Digital Editions: Lawrence & Wishart.

Engels, Frederick 1890, "Engels to C. Schmidt in Berlin", *Marx-Engels Correspondence*. https://www.marxists.org/archive/marx/works/1890/letters/90_08_05.htm

Heinrich, Michael 1996, "Engels' edition of the third volume of *Capital* and Marx's original manuscript", Science & Society 60 (4), pp.452–66.

Kapp, Yvonne 2018, *Eleanor Marx: A Biography*, New York: Verso.

Krätke, Michael 2020, "Friedrich Engels' politisches 'Testament'", *Zeitschrift für sozialistische Politik und Wirtschaft* (200 Jahre Engels), Heft 240, pp.59–64.

Küttler, Wolfgang, Alexis Petrioli and Frieder Otto Wolf 2004, "Historisch-kritische Wörterbuch des Marxismus", in *Historischer Materialismus*, ed. Wolfgang Fritz Haug, Berlin: Berliner Institut für kritische Theorie (InkriT).

Marx, Karl and Frederick Engels 2010, "Manifesto of the Communist Party", in *Marx & Engels Collected Works*, pp.477–519, Digital Editions: Lawrence & Wishart.

Moseley, Fred 2018, "Marx's Work on Volume III After 1865: Why Did Marx Not Finish Volume III?", in *The Unfinished System of Karl Marx: Critically Reading Capital as a Challenge for our Times*, ed. Judith Dellheim and Frieder Otto Wolf, pp.121–28, Cham: Springer International Publishing.

Teeple, Gary 1984, *Marx's Critique of Politics, 1842–1847,* Toronto: University of Toronto Press.

Wolf, Frieder Otto 2008, "Engels' Altersbriefe als philosophische Intervention: Worum ging es und mit welchen Mitteln hat Engels eingegriffen?", in *Beiträge zur Marx-Engels-Forschung, Neue Folge,* pp.140–56, Berlin: Berliner Verein zur Förderung der MEGA-Edition.

Wolf, Frieder Otto 2021, "Materialism against Materialism: Taking up Marx's Break with Reductionism", in *Materialism and Politics,* ed. B Bianchi, E Filion-Donato, M Miguel and A Yuva, Berlin: ICI Berlin Press.

Wolf, Frieder Otto 2023, *Finite Marxism: A collection of essays,* Leiden: Brill Historical Materialism (forthcoming).

INTERVIEW WITH ÁNXEL TESTAS

The Spanish left in transition: Interview with Anticapitalistas

Political developments in the Spanish state have been of intense interest to the left since the explosion of the Indignados movement in 2011. In the aftermath of the months-long occupations of public squares, a new political project emerged onto the scene, Podemos. While it started as a coalition between well-known media personalities and the far left, Podemos quickly achieved success and grew, alongside SYRIZA, into Europe's most prominent neo-reformist organisation. Marxist Left Review *and* Socialist Alternative *were highly critical of the Podemos leadership and their populist approach to politics, which quickly moved to smash any radicalism within their organisation.*[1] *Clearly, this was not a party that could seriously challenge the ruling class or their system. Yet as with SYRIZA, we were open to a range of tactical approaches to the new situation created by the rise of these new parties, insofar as the size, strength and political experience of revolutionaries was being developed in a clear and principled opposition to the reformist leaders.*

We are therefore happy to be publishing this interview with Ánxel Testas of Anticapitalistas, the largest Marxist organisation in the Spanish state. It was conducted following his visit to our Marxism Conference in Melbourne this year, and reflects on the questions raised

---

1. See Hassan 2016.

there with honesty and insight, from the perspective of an organisation that is continuing to fight to build the left and influence events as best they can. Of course, Anxel's views are his own, and are not necessarily shared by the editors or Socialist Alternative.

> *At the time it was formed Podemos was an inspiration to many on the international left. It seemed to signal a new possibility for consolidating the left and anti-austerity politics generated by the global financial crises. What was your role in the process of establishing the party, and what did you hope to accomplish?*

At the end of 2013, after two years of intense mobilisations in the streets following the outbreak of Indignados movement, a movement whose banner was a strong critique of the party system, there was a paradoxical situation: the struggles, despite their intensity, had not achieved victories and, on the other hand, the political landscape remained blocked. In 2014 there were European elections that heralded a timid rise of a United Left (a post-Eurocommunist organisation with an anti-neoliberal slant) that had undertaken a slight renewal. However, in Galicia and Catalonia (two historical nationalities within the Spanish state) new electoral experiences of the anti-capitalist left (the CUP in the Catalan case) and left-wing nationalism (Anova in the Galician case, together with a very small United Left) had achieved significant successes, and the experience of Syriza was also an important point of reference for us.

We detected the growing interest in politics (albeit in diffuse terms, between electoral and radical) after the mobilisations had stopped, and we tried to set up different initiatives from our limited forces, thinking more in the municipal terrain where there were important concentrations of activists where it would be easier to start. On a larger scale, we did not have a political agreement with Izquierda Unida [IU, United Left] to do something similar to the French Front de Gauche or Syriza, because of their refusal not to subordinate themselves to social liberalism (now it is hardly remembered, but in Andalusia, the biggest region in Spain, they participated in the regional government together with the PSOE [Spanish Socialist Workers' Party]) and there were no anti-capitalist organisations of sufficient scale for an anti-capitalist front (nor with the will to relate to real mass processes). For us it was fundamental to be able to make a leap in the political and social organisation of the movement (and within this broader process, the strengthening of our organisation).

At the end of 2013 the idea arose of trying to carry out an electoral experiment outside Izquierda Unida for the European elections (which, being a single constituency, allowed for experimentation), taking advantage of the increasingly well-known figure of Pablo Iglesias on television and trying to seek agreements with forces in the historic nationalities (which was not achieved). Despite this, we decided to give it a try, with us (Izquierda Anticapitalista, a revolutionary Marxist group of around 500 militants with a presence in different cities in Spain) and a group of activists and teachers, closely linked to the student movement in Madrid, around Pablo Iglesias (and immediately afterwards, also around Iñigo Errejón) as the promoters. Podemos was born, albeit diffusely, on the left and in competition with the reformist left, but without being a clearly anti-capitalist project.

Expectations soared within days of the public launch of the initiative in January. In February there were already mass meetings in almost every city in the state, organised in the form of circles. The social composition of these circles is much more working-class than that of the active nuclei of the Indignados movement, but activists from social movements, trade unionists and experienced left-wing cadres were generally absent. Our role was fundamental in generating a national structure to sustain the initiative, but the truth is that there is a logic of overflow in which it is enough for one person to make a meeting public on Facebook for it to fill up.

Our objectives were escalating at the same speed as the process was accelerating: from setting up a broad and plural political nucleus that aspires to electoral representation with a radical shock program, we were moving on to aspiring to set up a mass workers' party (with us being the militant nucleus of a radical wing) with possibilities of reaching the government (in June the polls showed Podemos as the first force), and to initiate a process of rupture with the 78 regime[2] and with the Europe of austerity, hoping to open a front together with Greece.

> *The party leadership campaigned against your existence as an organised tendency within Podemos very early on. Can you explain why Iglesias and his clique were so hostile to independent revolutionary organisation, and how you responded? What impact did this red-baiting have on the inner life of Podemos broadly, and your own position within it?*

The political and strategic conception of the Podemos leadership (self-constituted at the beginning around the media power of Pablo Iglesias) had two tributaries: post-Marxist populism via Latin America, and Eurocommunism: direct mass leader relations without intermediaries, the primacy of taking positions in the state, the acceptance of bourgeois institutional frameworks and, in the end, the postponement or direct refusal of the possibility of a socialist transformation of society led by the working class. These tendencies reached here paroxysmal and exaggerated levels: degradation of politics to communication and a vertical, militantly anti-pluralist and plebiscitary (click-through) organisational model. The grassroots structures lost all power, which was handed over to a network of arrogant and ridiculous General Secretaries who reproduced the superficial characteristics of the leader. The circles had no tasks beyond sticking up posters, nor economic resources or political decision-making capacity, they were a place for cheering the leadership.

This meant attacking the only organised and public organisation that existed in Podemos, and it was done viciously, taking advantage of the prejudices against political parties that existed in some of the people who participated. At that time, many militants of social and political movements, both of communist tradition and the autonomists, who had fought against the launching of Podemos, entered directly into the apparatus, blindly accepting the leadership and the dominant theses, and formed the cadres and elected deputies of the organisation.

2. The left describes the system established after the death of Franco as the 78 regime.

The impact on the internal life of Podemos was devastating, and in the long run a historical and generational catastrophe. The opportunity was missed to set up a genuine mass organisation – today there are hardly any activists who are not directly employed by the party. It generated a very arid terrain not only for our construction but also for minimum frameworks of debate, work and democratic culture. Thousands of people who went through the circles will never return to active politics.

As for our position as Anticapitalistas, it forced us to be very defensive and to strengthen ourselves politically, organisationally and materially. We also remained outside the national leadership (although it was never a democratic collegiate space) and we remained internally in a life increasingly limited to public current fights around the internal primaries and within the parliamentary groups. Without internal life and without strong social struggles, with practically all the young people outside the circles, we found it hard to identify fertile ground for growth and development of our tendency.

> *Given what you've described about the party structures becoming increasingly centralised and hollow, can you explain what participation in Podemos looked like? And how did you balance that with work outside the organisation: in street protests, workplaces, on campuses?*

Our presence in Podemos was on three fronts: 1) in the circles, where it was rapidly dying out, in part we were expelled and in part we abandoned them after only the fanatical supporters of the leadership remained; 2) in the institutional spaces where we had a presence; 3) in the internal life of the currents. These last two spheres, although totally fragmented by currents and with hardly any effective participation from below (although in the moments of activation of internal fights, hundreds of people and thousands of supporters were dragged along), had an outstanding public repercussion, turning the internal life into a public sphere of debates (through networks, articles, our own acts), but without any joint action. It should be made clear that we headed broad currents grouped under Anticapitalistas, but we were always careful to separate very clearly what Anticapitalistas was (a Marxist revolutionary organisation) and what those currents were. On the other side, there were the currents of Pablo Iglesias and Iñigo Errejón, which were only formally active in the primaries, but had no public or open organisational reality (they were more networks of internal and elected officials).

But it was not all Podemos. In 2015 there were municipal elections and elections in most of the autonomous communities (the Spanish state is divided into 17 autonomous communities). Podemos did not participate with its own brand in the municipal elections (for fear that it would detract their strength for the national elections), but this prudence opened up a more fertile field of hundreds of very different alliances at the local, and even autonomous community, levels. To give two examples: in the city of Madrid we presented ourselves in the municipal primaries on a list with activists from social movements and autonomy in a space that Podemos later joined *in extremis* in a negotiation from above (this platform won the government of the city); in Galicia the same thing happened at the regional level. Municipalism greatly enriched what was considered to be "the movement for change", which included parties such as Podemos and Izquierda Unida, and multiple spaces and platforms that could in turn contain these organisations and others, along with more people, with very different power relations and relative weights depending on the locality.

In terms of activity outside this "space of change", militant activity in general was much reduced. First of all, if we have already said that social struggles had begun to decline before the launch of Podemos (and could not be attributed to it), the growth of Podemos, the crisis of the party regime and of the monarchy (also due to the Catalan independence movement), the victory of Syriza in Greece and the achievement of government in the country's big cities, generated a rapid pendulum swing from, to quote Daniel Bensaïd, social illusion to electoral illusion. There was great expectation as to what could be achieved in this area. On the other hand, the leadership of Podemos made a very important contribution to crystallising this mood. Moreover, the economic situation had relatively stabilised and the hardest years of austerity were behind us, and the trade unions (from the majority to the most combative) played a very secondary and passive role during those years.

We used the slogan "one foot in the institutions, a thousand in the streets" and we also recovered the old Chilean slogan of "fight, create, popular power", insisting that a party-movement was necessary to strengthen itself socially and politically in order to be able to aspire to sustain a clash against the ruling class and its political regime. However, we did not have the strength to make this turn and the absence of social and trade union struggles created an absence of levers on which to rely.

As for our specific tasks, we tried to maintain and support the struggles that broke out from time to time, with the idea of lending resources and encouraging workers' self-organisation (against the fashion of the time, at the height of political communication and the narcissism of public officials, who went to demonstrations to take pictures of themselves). At the youth level we launched our own organisation (Abrir Brecha: Open the Gap) in the face of the growing disaffection of young leftists for professional politics, but the truth is that the situation on campus, after the defeat of the strong student movement of 2007–2009, was also very passive.

The one exception was the explosive rise of the women's movement, which brought about major change but remained outside party politics.

How did Anticapitalistas respond to the decision by Podemos to form a coalition government with PSOE?

When that decision was taken, we formalised our exit from Podemos. However, it was already an exit that had been foreseen since the outcome of the 2019 elections and Podemos' line in the subsequent general elections. In May 2019 municipal elections took place again, in which we managed to force the most left-wing sectors of IU to launch joint candidacies in some places (and in some places also including Podemos, but as a three-party agreement with Anticapitalistas as an actor of its own), with the idea of having an institutional wedge in a new cycle that would already be different, focused on tasks of mobilisation and getting rooted in the working class. However, almost no candidacy surpassed 5 percent (the limit for representation) and this put a brake on the constitution of a radical pole with an institutional presence, with the sectors furthest to the left leaving very weakened. The cycle was closed and the entry into government was the culmination of a whole series of previous political capitulations: the only way to achieve anything (and it was becoming less and less what was aspired to) was to govern with the PSOE, which was once again an ally. This is the new mantra of the bulk of the Spanish parliamentary left.

The government that was formed bore no resemblance whatsoever to the Latin American governments of Chávez or the first Evo [Morales], or even to a government of a social democracy in its youthful phase like that of Olof Palme. It was a government of senile social liberalism committed to capitalist management and the *diktats* of European finance. It is true that it opened up expectations in certain sectors at a time of shrinking horizons, which favoured the integration of organised nuclei of the movements into the ministerial orbit, what Gramsci calls the "extended state". However, its balance sheet is underwhelming: today the working class has no more social strength or better living conditions than when it began, and the door has been opened to a government with the extreme right within it.

Would you say that this experience has strengthened Anticapitalistas, politically or numerically? In retrospect, would you have done anything differently?

It is complicated to evaluate our involvement using only one parameter: Anticapitalistas is much stronger in public knowledge and as a political current with real insertion in national political life. We have gained in capacity for tactical development, in political-organisational experience of our cadres, in communicative skills and geographical expansion, in capacity for our own and original theoretical-practical elaboration within and in dialogue with international Marxism, in polemic capacity with other political currents. But if we measure it from the potential possibilities that opened up with the emergence of Podemos, the scenario leaves much to be desired. We gave a strong political battle, on a scale of hundreds of thousands of people, but we did not have sufficient strength, capacity or alliances, nor were we accompanied by a level of confrontation and social struggle sufficient to take the political leadership of the process away from Iglesias and his team. This defeat is not only ours but of more sectors, but it obviously conditions us. Our rupture with Podemos and our move to extra-parliamentarism in most of the country also significantly shrinks our field of work. However, having maintained coherence, having sown positions, and having maintained organisational and political independence allows us to endure and to prepare for new situations.

In numbers we increased our size in a humble way (with ups and downs), leaving with perhaps 30 percent more comrades than what we entered with. Unlike, for example, the Argentinian crisis of 2001, the process of the Indignados and Podemos did not generate an organised militant layer among the people who participated in it and that, together with other reasons, was also an important reason for the difficulty of growing qualitatively in numbers.

What would we have done differently? We should have had more visibility of our own when we launched Podemos, much less naivety towards the manoeuvres of the clique of Iglesias and Errejón, as well as having rejected the punctual pacts that we sometimes reached with Iglesias's faction to stop the right-wing turn of the organisation promoted by Errejón (once the alliance defeated Errejón, Iglesias applied precisely that policy).

> *You've recently written a long piece for the Spanish journal, Vientosur, titled "Points for militants reorienting themselves in slow times".[3] Can you summarise your main arguments and your organisation's perspectives for the coming period?*

Basically what I propose is that we need a strategic rearmament of the revolutionary left that, besides updating the strong theses (workers' government, united front, revolutionary party, transition program) goes through being able to find tactical initiatives that allow us to seek a serious implantation in the sectors of the working class of the twenty-first century with strategic strength. This varies a lot in each country, so

---

3.   Testas 2023.

it is necessary to undertake a rigorous study of the social formation and identify the levers of strength of the working class locally, rather than just applying general clichés. Having said this, the search for routes towards those sectors of the working class with strategic strength and the capacity to unite and lead the whole class behind them (the miners of the last century) implies a whole range of tactical developments, which in turn imply a change of methods, of languages and forms of work of a radical left often incapable of rethinking its repertoires (articles, debates in networks, appearance in demonstrations with its own banners). Sometimes the left can be more concerned with its prestige among its equally small competitors than with doing the more silent and less visible work of insertion among the class. With this I do not mean that maintaining the nuclei and the basic ideas of revolutionary Marxism is outdated, only that it is simply the starting point. But making leaps to transcend the necessary propaganda groups implies changes.

It is also necessary to have the will to develop political initiatives, which even if from extra-parliamentary positions, seek to speak to the whole society from the standpoint of the interest of the working class. There is a real risk that, as a comrade commented in a recent piece,[4] the revolutionary left remains in counter-cultural circles of young radicals or that it isolates the groups of radical workers from the rest of the class. To summarise schematically with a historical example: in the Chile of the Popular Unity [1970-73] the copper miners are the core sector of the class. The Chilean MIR, starting from a student/intellectual environment, is able to find a shortcut: it implants itself among the poor workers of the urban peripheries and from these positions it is able to provide itself with a social base with which to address the rest of the class. Not everything is straight lines. Obviously then there was a pre-revolutionary dynamic, but what is important is the way of open strategic thinking: how to break the isolation of the revolutionary left, thinking not only in terms of numbers but also in terms of strategic strength. This is just an example with many debatable points, but I believe it is necessary to get out of the rut and think boldly.

---

4. Fernandez 2023.

In Anticapitalistas we are trying to develop this, maintaining a work of public appearance and youth work (programmatic development, maintenance of nuclei, recruitment), and at the same time strengthening our presence and organic ties and accompanying experiences and struggles of young trade unionists in public health and in large industry where the question of eco-social transition begins to be talked about, seeking ways to approach strategic sectors of the working class and promoting union organisations in oppressed sectors of urban migrant workers involved in house-cleaning and care for the elderly.

> *Can you explain the relationship between Podemos and the left around Izquierda Unida and its offshoots? Were the forces around the old Communist Party any help in forming a principled left opposition to the Iglesias and Errejón cliques?*

IU (the "broad party" of the CP, almost all of whose members are CP) was in a moment of timid renewal when Podemos was born. Its first reaction was defensive. While it lost a number of core cadres to the Iglesias clique and, to a lesser extent, to the Errejón clique, IU made a strong rhetorical shift to the left in the 2015 general elections. Months later, the CP leadership reached an agreement with the Iglesias leadership and went hand in hand until this year, when they broke away and supported Sumar (the new personality-driven formation around the Minister of Labour and former CP militants). However, within the IU and within the CP there were different positions (sometimes reflected in a territorial way). Although the confederal leadership (that is, the state leadership, in the structure of which the federations of the autonomous communities, especially Andalusia, have strong weight) was an accomplice of the Iglesias clique, in important places like the government in Madrid, we maintained an alliance with them against the right-wing drifts of both Iglesias and Errejón cliques. This, as I said, ended in 2019 with a defeat that weakened them and their positions internally. Although the most left-wing sectors have fought hard within the CP (40 percent in the last congress), they have supported the line of government with the PSOE. In Andalusia, IU went so far as to secretly agree with the extreme right of Vox to expel us from the parliamentary group we shared (and where we were the majority), taking advantage of bureaucratic loopholes and the maternity leave of one of our comrades to win the vote.

> *Autonomist currents have traditionally been strong in Spain, a fact which was reflected in the widespread anti-party common sense of the Indignados movement. How did these tendencies respond to the Podemos leadership's overwhelmingly electoralist focus? Where do they sit today?*

These currents have many varieties that are difficult to homogenise and summarise, but I will try to describe some general processes. As far as trade union currents are concerned, they were absent from the Indignados struggle. At the political level, they were an important actor in the structuring of electoral candidacies at the municipal level in 2015, their preferred scale of work, especially in some of the country's large cities. Although they were reluctant at the launch of Podemos and elections, in general, they ended up integrating into the process a few months later. Their tradition lacks a history of strategic debates, which meant that while they were initially opposed to electoral politics, but suddenly when the tide went that way, they participated in it without any serious reflection. In places like Madrid, where they were a prominent political actor on the left (as a militant current and tradition rather than as an organic space), one sector quickly turned to populism and nourished Iñigo Errejón's clique with cadres, and others were our allies throughout the cycle, generating some of the most interesting criticisms of the process initiated by the Indignados movement (predominance of the middle classes) but at the same time, in my opinion, without offering much strategic clarity to go forward. Right now they are in crisis, as are many militant currents, with serious difficulties of generational renewal. They suffer greatly from the partial institutionalisation of part of the nuclei of the social movements (their main breeding ground), the police closure of social centres, the lack of social struggles and, in my opinion, their refusal to form stable and explicitly political organisations.

> *To examine more recent dynamics, could you give our readers*
> *some background to the rise of the far-right Vox party, as well*
> *as the hardening of the Popular Party's right wing?*

Vox is the expression of the arrival of the European extreme right's tide in Spain. Its growth has been facilitated by the defeats of the Catalan Independence Movement and Indignados-Podemos. It is in practice a split from the PP (which had always sheltered the most Francoist and fascist sectors of the right) and managed to make a leap after the rise of Spanish nationalism against Catalan independence after the referendum of 2017. At the same time they lead the opposition against feminism, thus embedding themselves in national dynamics and in those of the international alt-right. At its heart are sectors linked to big capital, as well as more locally oriented bourgeois and petty-bourgeois sectors, the common feature being that they were losers of globalisation (farmers, road transport companies, etc).

Vox's ability to make an electoral leap and polarise the debate has encouraged the PP to make a hard turn to the right, shifting its internal balance in favour of its most ultra wings, such as the PP of Madrid. But the PP is also obliged to maintain a more traditional-conservative profile in other regions, which causes them complicated breakdowns. The recent electoral non-victory of the right-wing parties may lead to a curious scenario of double "right-wingisation": Vox is in an important crisis due to the concern of the sectors of big capital that its presence will hinder clear majorities of the right. This can have the contradictory impact: the possible abandonment of the party by the sectors linked to financial capital could enable a turn towards more fascist positions within it. At the same time, the most radical sector of the PP has gained ground over the more traditional one, which has proven unable to defeat the left.

> *Anti-fascist slogans have historically had a strong resonance among the left and working class in the Spanish state, given the relatively recent experience of Franco's horrific dictatorship. How has the radical left responded to try and isolate and defeat Vox and other far right forces in the Spanish state? Did the catastrophic victory of Meloni in Italy spark new interest in this issue?*

The electoral leap of Vox after the elections in Andalusia in 2018 provoked dynamics of occasional mobilisations and counter-calls against Vox acts, etc. However, a good part of the parliamentary left and the majority unions opt at all times for a strategy of not feeding the troll and reject mobilisation. At the same time, they abuse the fear generated by the extreme right to justify support for PSOE as the lesser evil. The street mobilisations are relatively perfunctory and never acquire a mass character. Although they serve to contain the public presence of Vox in certain places, they are not able to represent a serious counterweight to stop its ongoing rise.

The rise of Vox means a certain increase in harassment and violence, especially towards LGTBI people and migrants. But what has increased the most is a certain level of daily harassment and the emboldening of reactionary sectors. In this area, it is the feminist movement that has had the greatest capacity to react and respond, especially young women who see a worrying increase in machismo and right-wing politics among young men. Interestingly, there is yet to be a rise in far-right squads and fascist grouplets as is classically described, but there is a dangerous dynamic expressed through the fascistisation of the police, their unions, and the judiciary. This translates into significant increases in police and judicial repression, including prison sentences for trade unionists or militants who have mobilised against Vox. This has posed additional difficulties to classic anti-fascist strategies.

Meloni's victory has not meant a rearmament of the mobilisations against the extreme right, but I believe that, together with the conformation of autonomous and municipal governments of Vox-PP in June 2023, it has indirectly contributed to the electoral mobilisation in the general elections of July that, although it has been fundamentally towards the PSOE and then Sumar, has been provoked beyond a framing around the need to stop the far right.

> *Inflation, driven in large part by corporate profiteering, has seen a huge attack on working class living standards across the world. How has the PSOE-Podemos-IU coalition responded to this critical situation, and what is their relationship to the austerian institutions of the EU?*

The truth is that the European ruling class learned the lessons of the previous crisis – and of the whole cycle of revolts of the last years – and has not for now launched a frontal attack against the working class, because of political reservations and also because their bourgeoisies need an injection of public funds due to their structural difficulties in maintaining their profits. Sectors like the automobile industry literally live on this. This has generated something similar to what Brenner calls "military Keynesianism, without growth or redistribution", which has resulted, in the Spanish state, with brutal increases in military spending and with an injection of bailout funds which have basically gone into the pockets of big business, but have also allowed the financing of temporary packages of measures designed to palliate the most extreme situations. However, what the coalition government sells as a "big social shield", is in reality temporary crumbs, which inflation leaves for nothing, and which deepen indebtedness which, in the face of the refusal to address a conflict with the elites over the distribution of wealth or at least a far-reaching tax reform, undermines the possibilities for structuralising these poor measures and will prepare the ground for more drastic adjustments.

> *If PSOE and their allies manage to hold on to power, what do you see as the potential flashpoints for class and social struggles in the next period?*

Right now there are no clear elements to be able to make a firm forecast. The political plane is in a very tense equilibrium on very shaky ground (the small nationalist groupings might form a pact with PSOE and

Sumar), which nevertheless has the real effect of partially paralysing social struggles. An imbalance on this plane can change the panorama of the class and social struggles, in the sense of displacing obstacles (friendly government syndrome, union contention, lobbying by the social movement's organisations, national question) or also diluting illusions in the government's capacity to undertake structural changes. However, I also do not think that we should have too much hope that an eventual change in the political and economic situation of the country would lead to an automatic reaction of the working class. The strategy of containment and co-option deployed by reformist politicians and union bureaucracies also has long term repercussions on the capacity of these actors to respond, and even the most dynamic sectors that remain outside the orbit of the friendly government are weak.

There are tough union struggles for wages in classic industrial sectors, and others in new sectors (cleaning, department stores) which are ending with partial victories and draws, but none have a major impact on the national political landscape. The citizens' struggles and workers' strikes in defence of the public health system are still going on without either victories or crushing defeats, as is the struggle of the pensioners. It seems likely that they will continue, as health and pension funds are the last great economic niches still to be exploited by European and North American capitalists. All these sectors have not yet suffered a general defeat and I believe that we can expect some response from them. Similarly, the ecological and feminist movements, although having been through organisational crises, continue to enjoy mass support and are relatively powerful on a mass level.

Once the financial resources of the EU that are sustaining the profits of uncompetitive companies and government aid for the poor run out, which they will, there will inevitably be harsher adjustment plans. We need to study the medium-term plans of the European bourgeoisie and be attentive to the real developments of the class struggle, and be prepared to take advantage of the interregnum. Finally, in the face of the political weakness of the workers' movement, we should not rule out social explosions through non-traditional channels, like the yellow vests in France.

References

Fernandez, Brais 2023, "El impase español", *Jacobin*, 18 May. https://jacobinlat.com/2023/05/18/el-impase-espanol/

Hassan, Omar 2016, "Podemos and left populism", *Marxist Left Review*, 11, Summer. https://marxistleftreview.org/articles/podemos-and-left-populism/

Testas, Ánxel 2023, "Apuntes militantes para reorientarse en tiempos lentos", *VientoSur*, 186, 10 March. https://vientosur.info/apuntes-militantes-para-reorientarse-en-tiempos-lentos/

LUCA TAVAN

Review: The rise of the far right in Italy

Luca Tavan has been involved in campaigns against education cuts, for refugee rights, and in solidarity with Palestine. He has written extensively on Italy's *Biennio Rosso* and "Hot Autumn".

David Broder, *Mussolini's Grandchildren: Fascism in Contemporary* Italy, Pluto Press, 2023.

THE ITALIAN GENERAL election at the end of 2022 was a historic win for the far right. A coalition of the three major right-wing parties won 44 percent of the vote, enough in Italy's byzantine electoral system to form a clear majority in both houses of parliament. Most importantly, it was driven by the meteoric rise of Giorgia Meloni's Brothers of Italy (Fratelli d'Italia, Fd'I), a party rooted in the post-Mussolini fascist tradition, which secured 26 percent of the vote, making it the single largest party in parliament. Meloni was able to form a government in coalition with the far right Lega and Forza Italia, the party of recently deceased and infamously corrupt media magnate Silvio Berlusconi.

Mussolini's Grandchildren: Fascism in Contemporary Italy, by left-wing journalist and historian David Broder, details the history of Meloni's Brothers of Italy, and its predecessor parties.

Giorgia Meloni entered politics as a teenager, joining the neo-fascist Italian Social Movement (MSI) in the 1990s. A 1996 French TV program interviewed the 19-year-old, who told them: "I think Mussolini was a good politician. He did what he did for Italy. There haven't been other politicians like him these last fifty years" (p.101). At this time, the MSI was still led by ageing cadres of Mussolini's Salo Republic, who had fought alongside the Nazis in the last days of World War Two and had never renounced the dictatorship they had served.

Meloni launched Fratelli d'Italia in 2012, alongside other MSI leaders, as a continuation of that tradition, symbolised by their adoption of the old MSI insignia, the *tricolore* flame. In her memoir, she writes of the moment Fd'I moved into the old MSI headquarters in Rome:

> I remain silent, and suddenly I realise the enormous responsibility I have taken on. I picked up the baton of a seventy-year-long history, I carried on my shoulders the dreams and hopes of a people who found themselves without a party, who had risked going astray. It's as if those millions of people are still here, all those fighting with me today and those who are no longer here. As if they were looking at me, silently asking, "are you up to the task". (p.48)

Some elements of Meloni's reputation were barriers to her acceptance among the European political establishment – but not her celebration of fascist dictators or threats to expel migrants. The ruling class feared only that Meloni might not adhere to the "two A's" necessary to enter the European club – "Atlanticism and austerity" as Benoît Bréville put it in an article for *Le Monde diplomatique*.[1] On the campaign trail, Fratelli candidates were far more frequently interrogated about these positions than about the party's fascist heritage or reactionary social positions.

Since reaching office Meloni has shown her commitment to NATO and demanded further sanctions on Russia, while preparing an austerity budget and slashing welfare spending. This was clearly enough to win over European Commission President Ursula von der Leyen, once a sceptic and now a cheerleader for Fratelli. After an initially icy reception from Emanuel Macron at the end of 2022, the pair now pose for photos outside the Élysée Palace.

---

1.   Bréville 2023.

Nearly a year since Fratelli's election, there are many projecting Italy's government as a model for the right. Alexander Downer, foreign minister for 12 years under Liberal Prime Minister John Howard, was starstruck upon meeting Meloni recently in London. "As things stand Meloni has the potential to become the European Union's most significant leader." He notes the shift in the political climate which has allowed Meloni to play a role:

> Europe outside the UK is gradually drifting to the right. Already conservatives are entrenched in Hungary and Poland. The Dutch government is a longstanding centre-right coalition which is now under attack from a new right-wing farmers' movement. Sweden and Finland have both recently ousted left-wing governments.[2]

Barriers that once separated the traditional centre-right and far right are collapsing. As mainstream conservative forces like the British Tories, US Republicans and Hungarian Prime Minister Viktor Orbán's Fidesz radicalise to the right, and fascist outfits have succeeded in making breakthroughs by promoting themselves as part of the mainstream, how do we understand Fratelli d'Italia? Are they still fascists, and what does it mean for them to be in a position to form governments and shape the political landscape?

In tracing the lineage of Fd'I back to the postwar MSI and attempting to explain the tradition's long march from the margins of politics to the halls of power, *Mussolini's Grandchildren* gives valuable insights into the meaning of Meloni's government. The history it provides shows that the Italian fascists never went away, and that the process of normalisation and incorporation into the political system goes back decades. Italian fascists had many accomplices – from street-fighting hooligans, to conservative intellectuals, to prime ministers, media magnates and bourgeois historians. This review will summarise the most valuable arguments of Broder's book, address a few of its limitations, and then attempt to draw some conclusions from the first period of Meloni's government.

---

2.   Downer 2023.

Meloni's progenitors: "Fascists in a democracy"

Chapter 3 explains how the MSI was founded at the end of 1946 by stalwarts of the fallen Salo Republic, defined by leader Giorgio Almirante as a party of "fascists in a democracy". Italian fascism emerged from the ruins of World War Two battered and bloodied, but not vanquished. They struggled to find a place in the postwar Italian Republic, which was shaped by the collective memory of the resistance, while maintaining the continuity of their fascist tradition.

Under new leader Augusto de Marsanich from 1950, the MSI pursued a "strategy of insertion", attempting to build themselves as a credible anti-Communist ally of the ruling Christian Democracy (DC). This meant a revision of some deeply held positions – fascists who had just years ago fought militarily against the Allied invasion of Italy now endorsed the NATO alliance and oriented toward Washington in the name of fighting the red menace. Centre-right Christian Democrats, who governed Italy alongside various junior coalition partners from the late 1940s to the early 1990s, accepted the fascists as a legitimate party. Yet the MSI were never able to be incorporated into government. This was most dramatically expressed in 1960, when a new DC-led government under Fernando Tambroni became reliant on MSI votes to secure a majority, breaking the established pattern of excluding the party from power. When it was announced that the MSI would hold their national conference in Genoa, a mass demonstration and general strike of semi-insurrectionary proportions took place, toppling the government and reimposing the MSI's isolation. So it was not the establishment who ensured the MSI were kept to the parliamentary margins – it was the workers' movement and the left.

In 1969, amid the political polarisation created by the militant struggles of the "hot autumn",[3] the more radical Almirante took over the leadership, bringing neo-fascist groups that had abandoned the party back into the fold. Broder points out that the MSI pursued a two-track strategy, emphasising law and order and respect for democratic institutions in public, while keeping open lines of communication

---

3.   For an overview of this period see Tavan 2023b.

with explicitly anti-democratic forces. Almirante himself described this approach as combining "the cudgel and the double-breasted suit".

In the early 1970s, in response to militant social struggle, sections of the state adopted the "strategy of tension", collaborating with small fascist terrorist organisations to carry out attacks which could be pinned on the left to justify repression. The most notorious of these, the 1969 Piazza Fontana bombing, was orchestrated by Ordine Nuovo, the group led by former MSI member Pino Rauti. While denouncing political violence in public, Almirante allegedly told MSI youth activists that their party and the terrorist organisations fought "the same battle in different trenches" (p.70). In Milan's Piazza San Babila, MSI activists mixed with the alphabet soup of small, clandestine fascist organisations. Most shockingly, Broder recounts how the investigation into one right-wing terror attack – a fascist car-bombing in Friuli in 1972 which killed three – directly implicated Almirante as a collaborator, although parliamentary immunity meant that he never faced charges.

Broder's history is an important contribution towards understanding the dynamism of far-right organisation. Through an Italian prism, Broder unveils the long history of political and personal entwinement between "respectable" far-right politicians and "extra-parliamentary" fascist thugs. It is commonplace today for commentators to attempt to draw strict lines of demarcation between the acceptable "electoral" far right who respect democratic institutions, and explicitly anti-democratic fascists who long for totalitarian rule.

This is also accepted by many on the left today. A recent article by US socialist Charlie Post makes a version of this argument: urging a distinction between "right-wing populism" which "relies primarily on electoral politics", and "fascism...a social movement that recruits members and builds power through violence and terror".[4] The problem with this argument is that it is well nigh impossible to clearly demarcate which forces on the far right will, as Post puts it, "bow to legality" in the last instance. As Broder argues:

> [B]ecause neofascists are able to run in elections does not

---

4.   Post 2023.

> mean there has been a straightforward pacification of these militants, some of whom have murdered, beaten and harassed ethnic minorities and left-wing activists in recent years, motivated by the same conspiracy theories which appear in their campaign materials. (p.117)

Trump's putsch of 6 January 2021 ended in farce, but hardly speaks to a concern for democratic procedure. Hungary's Orbán and India's Modi have both built their political careers through leading successful electoral vehicles, but both have already dramatically changed the terrain of politics and narrowed the democratic space in their respective states. Historically, too, an electoral focus is no guarantee of good democratic credentials; it has been a central element of every serious fascist force in history, from Mussolini's PNF, to Hitler's NSDAP, to the British National Front.

The most crucial difference between the modern far right and their precursors is that today they are operating in a wildly different political context. Classical fascism came to power in Italy and Germany in the interwar period, amid the deepest social crisis capitalism has ever faced, a period when the ruling class was faced by a revolutionary workers' movement which had shown its capacity to shake their rule. This stirred up deeply reactionary forces, radicalised right-wingers and created a receptivity to extreme undemocratic methods among the ruling class.

The fact that there are now political figures at the heads of state across the world like Meloni and Modi who include fascist dictatorships as part of their political tradition should not be taken lightly. Broder points to Meloni's own predecessors in the MSI to prove this point. Even as its leaders pledged acceptance of the Italian Republic, the MSI's commitment to bourgeois democracy was extremely conditional. After the 1973 Pinochet coup in Chile, Almirante declared that such a regime was also a valid option for Italy, while the MSI also openly championed the anti-Communist dictatorships in Spain, Portugal and Greece.

Into the mainstream

Much of Broder's analysis of the rise of Meloni's party hinges on the massive tectonic shift which took place in Italian politics in the 1990s. The MSI had spent four decades on the margins, constrained by the existing political system dominated by the centre-right Christian Democrats and the reformist Communist Party (PCI). Suddenly, with the fall of the Berlin Wall in 1989, this system collapsed. As the USSR began to break up, the PCI went into terminal crisis, voting to dissolve in 1991. Then the Christian Democrats and Socialist Party both fell after a wave of corruption scandals.

The first to step into this breach was Silvio Berlusconi, the venal Milanese media magnate, who launched the right-wing Forza Italia in late 1993, winning a general election just a few months later. Berlusconi pitched his party as a rearguard action against the return of remnants of the defeated Communist Party, and promised a Thatcherite revolution. In searching for right-wing allies, he decided it was possible and desirable to finally bring the MSI into the fold. He would later brag that he "invented the centre-right in 1994" by working "the League and the fascists" – "we legitimised and constitutionalised them".[5]

The new MSI leader Gianfranco Fini, who pledged to be a "fascist for the year 2000", jumped at the opportunity to realise the MSI's long-held objective of "insertion", forming Alleanza Nazionale (National Alliance) as an electoral front, and entering government for the first time. The fascists were now operating in a far more permissive intellectual climate. With the collapse of the party framework established in the aftermath of the Italian Resistance, the space was cleared for the right to challenge the dominant "anti-fascist" assumptions of the postwar period. A tidal wave of revisionist historiography was unleashed, based on the claim, as historian Renzo De Felice put it, that "the history of fascism was somehow taken hostage by the culture of the Italian left, hegemonized by the (Communist Party)".[6] Revisionist historians popularised the claims that anti-fascist partisans were just as violent and reprehensible as their fascist opponents and that Italian fascism had a basically positive record, its sole mistake being the decision

5.   Broder 2022.
6.   Quoted in Prezioso 2023.

to ally with Hitler. Echoing this argument, Berlusconi told Britain's *Spectator* in 2003: "Mussolini never killed anyone, he sent people into confinement to have vacations".[7]

The MSI tradition had long called for a process of "pacification" – the freeing of Italian history from polarisation between fascism and anti-fascism. Fratelli today often claim that they have "consigned fascism to the past". Rather than expressing some desire to break with the past, this is an injunction to Fratelli's critics to stop talking about fascism's historical crimes. After entering government for the first time in 1995, the MSI's Fiuggi Congress formally embraced liberal democracy, but asserted their continuity with a "right that had lived before, during and after the 1920s" (p.9).

Under Fini, Alleanza Nazionale participated in two coalition governments, the first in 1994 and the second from 2001–6, finally achieving the "insertion" into the political landscape they desired. But the process of incorporation provoked sharp debates within the party. By 2009 Fini was leading the process of dissolving Alleanza Nazionale into Berlusconi's party. Then, in 2010 the Eurozone crisis hit Italy, and the "Troika" of the European Commission, the European Central Bank (ECB) and the International Monetary Fund (IMF) forced Berlusconi to resign, appointing a "technocratic" national unity government.

Fratelli pick up the torch

These two developments led to Meloni, alongside former Berlusconi ally Guido Crosseto, to split and form Fratelli d'Italia in 2012. From the start, the project sought to re-establish the continuity of fascist identity which had been consciously diluted by Fini. This should warn us against naive claims that participation in electoral politics and even government means that fascists are being gradually and progressively "domesticated".

> [I]t is not the case that their ability to participate in democratic forums has broken their tie to fascism. Rather...they bring

---

7. Quoted in Ben-Ghiat 2022.

fascist ideas into mainstream platforms and even institutional settings. (p.117)

Fratelli have risen amid the social decay and misery caused by neoliberalism and obsessive fiscal austerity which have been pursued vigorously by both the centrist Democratic Party and the right. Italy spends more on servicing the interest on its debt than it does on public education. On average, workers have got poorer since the turn of the century and are less likely to be able to find work. Broder only spends a couple of pages exploring neoliberalism, which could have been expanded, but he draws some important conclusions about its political consequences, writing:

> This decline of Italians' attachment to political parties has not produced a return of the social conflict that had dissipated in the 1980s. Rather, the result has been an increasingly volatile electoral politics, through the rise of "outsiders" who channel anger but also express lowered expectations of what kind of change is even possible", but also noting "the normalisation of the idea that political decisions stand above democratic choice." (p.144)

Perhaps the most consequential decision of the new party was to refuse, unlike Berlusconi and the far-right Lega, to support the technocratic government led by the banker Mario Monti. The perception that Fd'I stood outside of this establishment was central to Meloni's rise; she was elected at the end of 2022 after the collapse of yet another "national unity" government, this time led by Mario Draghi. Again, Meloni's party refused to support the unelected austerity government. Draghi's record as the former head of the ECB is notorious. During the Eurozone crisis from 2009, he threatened Greece with economic strangulation after the election of Syriza on an anti-austerity platform.

Fratelli's steady rise over the past decade has also been facilitated by a competition on the right to both promote and capitalise on anti-immigrant sentiment. Both Meloni and the far-right Lega's Mateo Salvini have threatened mass deportations of migrants, attacked NGOs that conduct rescue operations in the Mediterranean and embraced

Renaud Camus' "great replacement" theory. This was reinforced by the racism of the political centre – the Democratic Party has utilised the right-wing slogan "Let's help them in their own country" in the context of immigration debates.

The long-term normalisation of far-right and fascist outfits of different stripes has created a diverse milieu within which Fratelli mixes. Chapter 5 of Broder's book makes for disturbing reading, as he covers the broad spectrum from the "hipster-fascists" of Casa Pound who operate from an occupied social centre on Rome's Via Napoleone III, to the fascists of the football club Hellas Verona who display Nazi flags at games. While many of these activists and thugs are not members of Fratelli, there are innumerable personal and organisational links that tie them together. In 2018, one such activist opened fire on African migrants in the town of Macerata, killing six. It was later revealed he had been a candidate for the far-right Lega, one of the parties in Meloni's coalition. While Meloni equivocated and attempted to obscure the clear political motive behind the attack, she was far from equivocal in her condemnation of the subsequent anti-fascist demonstration by outraged citizens in the town.

Fratelli emerged as the leading force on the Italian right in the run-up to the 2022 election. Meloni was able to cannibalise the voting base of her coalition partners, Lega and Berlusconi's Il Popolo della Libertà. Fratelli benefitted from its outsider status – both Lega and PdL were electorally damaged by their participation in Draghi's unity government. But while many portrayed their rise as a meteoric breakthrough, Broder's book shows that the conditions for Meloni's government were laid over decades. On the one hand, it was the result of decades of fascist cadre organising in the MSI and Alleanza Nazionale, those who "kept the flame alive" even in periods of marginality. On the other, they were able to insert themselves because of a toxic political climate increasingly permissive of fascist politics.

Whatever happened to the Italian left?

The most glaring weakness of Broder's book is the way it elides any serious discussion of the Italian left, its political divisions and its eventual catastrophic collapse. Italy was once host to one of the biggest lefts in the developed world. It's impossible to gain a full understanding of the strength of the Italian right without reference to the failures of the left, in particular the Italian Communist Party, the hegemonic left organisation in Italy from the Resistance during World War Two until the 1990s.

Broder does note in chapter 3 that for the political survival of fascist forces, "A key turning point came in June 1946, when [Communist] justice minister Palmiro Togliatti granted an amnesty for a swathe of wartime crimes, including 'collaborationism'". That is, the leader of the Italian Communist Party held a key ministry immediately after the war and used his position to show clemency to fascist war criminals. The author acknowledges that this decision allowed future MSI leaders like Almirante to come out of clandestinity and establish a new organisation. Yet Broder neglects to interrogate the context for this extraordinary approach.

Communist Party members had been the backbone of the Italian resistance to Nazi occupation.[8] But the leadership of the PCI pursued a fundamentally conservative strategy, the application to Italy of Stalin's Popular Front. The real motive of this policy was the subordination of the party to Russian imperialist interests, at this time shaped by a hostility to workers' revolution and the exigencies of military alliance with Britain and the US. They justified this with a stageist theory: national liberation first, deferring the question of fighting for socialism to an undefined future date. As historian Paul Ginsborg notes, the effect was "to dissipate the strength of the resistance and of worker and peasant agitation".[9]

In a move that shocked many Communist militants, Togliatti announced in 1944 that the party would move out of opposition and join the Allied-backed government, headed by the fascist army general Badoglio and the king. The Allies made it clear that their fundamental priority was not a thoroughgoing purge of the fascists from the state apparatus, but stability and continuity. As militant workers in the north liberated cities with mass strikes and insurrections, in the south the Allies were prioritising keeping together the state bureaucracy

8.   Vassiley 2022.
9.   Ginsborg 1990, p.47.

inherited from fascism. While anti-fascists pushed for a cleansing of the state, the judiciary went untouched, and most leading fascist apparatchiks kept their jobs. Ginsborg writes that even as late as 1960, 62 of 64 provincial prefects were fascist functionaries, as were all of the country's 135 police chiefs.[10]

Togliatti's light-touch approach to prosecuting fascists in the postwar period has to be set in the context of the PCI's class-collaborationist political strategy. This was a decision with enormous consequences. It provided the fascists a lifeline, and allowed them to bury themselves in the state apparatus. This is the reason why, by the time the struggles of the late 1960s broke out, fascist groups who wanted to wage armed terror against the left could still find collaborators in the highest reaches of the security establishment.

Broder pinpoints the collapse of the PCI in 1991 as an important moment in the rise of the right; the mass party had been "one of the main champions of anti-fascist memory culture" (p.29). Unfortunately he doesn't ask what internal limitations contributed to the party's spectacular implosion. Any rounded account of the rise of the right has to explain the collapse of the left.

Italy was once host to a mass socialist working-class movement, stretching from the reformist Communists and Socialists to a formidable range of revolutionary organisations which built an audience in the struggles of the hot autumn in 1969.[11] Most of these latter groups failed to survive the downturn in struggle which began in the mid-1970s. Their disappearance was followed a decade later by the dissolution of the PCI. Today, the absence of any credible left that has a national presence is one of the major reasons the far right has experienced such success, and faced so little resistance.

The immediate trigger for the collapse of the PCI was undeniably the shattered illusions produced by the fall of the USSR. But 1991 was so catastrophic precisely because the party had been through decades of decline. By the time of the struggles of the hot autumn, the party was already seen by a layer of student radicals, socialist intellectuals and some militant workers as irredeemably conservative and reformist

---

10. Ginsborg 1990, p.92.
11. For the decline of the revolutionary left, see Tavan 2023a.

in its orientation. After decades of a "two-track" approach, combining formal commitment to socialist revolution with reformist practice, the polarisation of the 1970s forced the PCI leadership to clarify its project. By 1978 they were championing law and order while reaching a "historic compromise" with Christian Democracy, backing a DC government while it implemented brutal austerity. Through the 1980s the Communist Party supported anti-strike laws and endorsed Italian participation in NATO.[12] Given this trajectory, it's unsurprising that at the PCI's Congress in 1991 the majority faction argued to dissolve and form the Party of the Democratic Left, a centre-left outfit which eventually morphed into the modern neoliberal Democratic Party.

The postwar left got a second wind with the emergence of Rifondazione Comunista (Communist Refoundation). Rifondazione was formed by the minority wing of the PCI who rejected the dissolution of their tradition, but it really took off when it jagged leftwards and played a substantial role in the mass anti-capitalist movement in the late 1990s. At the time, many commentators on the left championed Rifondazione's pluralistic and broad political make-up as the source of its strength.[13] While this might have been part of its appeal, it also meant there was never a serious reckoning with the strategic questions that had shipwrecked its predecessors. What should be said about the legacy of the PCI, its class-collaborationist strategy and popular-frontism? Did this new party stand for the overthrow of capitalism, or aspire to a share of state power? Ultimately this unresolved ambiguity played to the advantage of the party's reformist wing. By 2006 the party had shifted back to the right, and ended up in coalition with the centrist Democrats, voting to attack workers and to send troops into Afghanistan. This extremely discrediting experience led to Rifondazione's abandonment by its base and its collapse into obscurity.

David Broder is a historian of the Italian and French Communist Parties, whom nobody would accuse of ignorance of these developments. But the failure to integrate the lessons of this history into an account of the rise of the far right is an important omission. The subsequent political vacuum which was created by the failures of these

---

12. Behan 1999.
13. For a critique of the "broad party" strategy, see Armstrong 2014.

parties is essential to understanding the rise of the right. This wasn't inevitable, but was the fruit of the dead-end approaches of Stalinism and reformism. The failure to explain this gives an edge of fatalism to Broder's account of the right's success.

There is also little reference to the struggles from below which have framed Italian politics for the past eight decades. While there is a fleeting account of the 1960 anti-fascist uprising which emanated from Genoa, the radical struggles of 1968–78 are barely mentioned ("hot autumn" does not appear in the index). This reinforces the bleak impression that Broder's book leaves readers with. While Broder explores the responses from politicians and media to the fascist attack on CGIL headquarters in 2021, the anti-fascist demonstrations involving tens of thousands the following week are omitted. While left-wing political forces are in no position to decisively challenge Meloni at this point, it's important to point out that resistance *does* exist, from LGBTI+ and migrant rights activism, to transit and gas worker strikes against Meloni's economic agenda. The crucial task of the left is to build a credible political alternative that can unite and generalise these struggles.

How bleak is Italy's future?

In his conclusion, Broder summarises that Fratelli are not simply nostalgists, but have to be understood as a dynamic force of the modern right: "postfascism is not just a matter of a 'return to the past'. The far right is in power in new times, writing new history for the bearers of the *tricolore* flame" (p.176).

Since the publication of the book, what conclusions can we draw about what sort of right Meloni is forging? The first thing that has to be noted is that Meloni's coalition has been remarkably stable thus far. Many predicted that it would be short-lived – both because of the "irregular" politics of its main constituent party, and because most parliamentary coalitions tend to be fragile.

Crucially, Meloni's coalition has won the confidence of the business establishment. Guido Crosetto, president of a branch of the national employers' federation, Confindustria, has acted as an important interlocutor between the government and capital. Those who label forces like Meloni's "populist" and crudely assert that this inherently pairs with a protectionist and welfarist agenda aimed at a chauvinist working-class base will be surprised by Meloni's economic agenda. The core of it has been support for fiscal austerity, aimed at shoring up support from big business and continuing to access EU recovery funds negotiated by the previous government. Meloni promises to bolster national competitiveness with an economy based on low wages, low taxes and low spending. Already her government has attacked welfare and slashed compensation for victims of workplace accidents.

Far from merely ruling as a traditional centre-right party, the mark of Fratelli's political heritage has been felt from day one. Key ministries were renamed to express their ethno-nationalist worldview. The economic planning office was renamed "Ministry of Businesses and Made in Italy", the Equality and Families brief had "and Birth Rates" added to the end – fitting from a prime minister who believes there is a global conspiracy to ethnically displace Italians. While Meloni has been able to ingratiate herself with the European establishment by championing the NATO line on Ukraine, this has sat slightly uneasily with her support for Orbán's ostracised government in Hungary. Meloni's attempts to unify the right at a European level by bringing together the main parliamentary groupings (the Eurosceptic European Conservatives and Reformists, and the pro-Europe European People's Party) have been bedevilled by divisions over EU integration and Putin's invasion.

As part of her election campaign, Meloni threatened a naval blockade as the only way to address the "crisis" of refugees entering Italy. The government has retreated from this proposal, perhaps partly in response to her coalition partner Salvini being put on trial for blocking the entry of migrant boats while serving as interior minister in a previous government.[14]

Instead, Meloni is pursuing more conventional legal means to attack refugees and migrants. In the aftermath of the tragic sinking of a migrant boat off the coast of Calabria in May, which claimed 89 lives, a sweeping bill was passed increasing penalties for people smugglers, and making deportation easier.[15] At the same time, a series of laws

14. BBC 2021.
15. Fondation Robert Schuman 2023.

have been passed making it harder for NGOs to carry out life-saving rescue operations.[16]

Meloni, who last year exclaimed at a rally for Spain's far right Vox party: "Yes to natural families, no to the LGBT lobby, yes to sexual identity, no to gender ideology, yes to the culture of life, no to the abyss of death",[17] has launched an as yet unconsolidated offensive against LGBTI+ rights. Same-sex adoption and surrogacy have both emerged as targets, products of a gender ideology that according to Meloni seeks "the disappearance of women and the end of maternity".[18]

On the domestic front, one of Meloni's most ambitious projects of political reform is the introduction of a presidential system. This demand has echoed through the whole history of postwar Italian fascism, dating back to the 1960s when the MSI urged the creation of a more centralised political system on the French model: a strong state which could act decisively against external enemies and internal subversion.

Taken overall, Meloni's government has been able to rule successfully, operating on the terrain of Italian and European institutions while exerting influence on the politics of the present and future. Fratelli d'Italia have continued the long-term postwar strategy of insertion into the political sphere, and adapted to a relatively stable liberal-democratic order. At the same time, they've managed to maintain a continuity of fascist politics – points of reference which still guide their die-hard activists today. The stability of Italian society and lack of a working-class challenge mean that, unlike in the classical fascist period, violent street politics play at best an auxiliary role in Fratelli's project. There is nothing compelling the current government to carry out sweeping changes to the structure of state, or wage war on independent civil society. Nevertheless, Fratelli cadre are operating in a political climate that is more accommodating to advancing fascist politics than anything the MSI could have dreamed of in the postwar period. The history of the Italian far right should warn us against any

16. Bonnel 2023.
17. Balmer 2022.
18. Broder 2023.

complacent wish that Fratelli d'Italia have reached the limit of their political ambition.

Conclusion

Mussolini's Grandchildren is an important intervention into contemporary politics. As far-right and fascist forces continue to make breakthroughs across Europe, the book can help arm socialists with the history to make sense of our current moment and arguments against the tidal wave of whitewashing and normalisation that has allowed Fratelli to thrive. *Mussolini's Grandchildren* also reads as a searing indictment of capitalist politics, outlining how mainstream forces – technocratic politicians, right-wing historians and slimy media outlets – have all contributed to the current nightmare.

Unfortunately, Broder's book doesn't explore the successes and failures of the Italian left to draw lessons about the politics we need to confront the right today. The most important lesson we can draw from history, from the armed anti-fascist units of the *Arditi del Popolo* in the 1920s to the World War Two-era partisans, is that the fascists *can* be resisted. This is something missing from *Mussolini's Grandchildren*.

References

Armstrong, Mick 2014 "A critique of the writings of Murray Smith on broad left parties", *Marxist Left Review*, 7, Summer. https://marxistleftreview.org/articles/a-critique-of-the-writings-of-murray-smith-on-broad-left-parties/

Balmer, Crispian 2022 "Nationalist Meloni set to smash Italy's glass ceiling, become premier", *Reuters*, September 26. https://www.reuters.com/article/italy-election-meloni-idAFKBN2QR02P

BBC 2021, "Matteo Salvini: Right-wing Italy politician on trial for blocking migrant boat", October 23. https://www.bbc.com/news/world-europe-59020839

Behan Tom 1999, "The Return of Italian Communism?", *International Socialism*, 2:84, Autumn. https://www.marxists.org/history/etol/newspape/isj2/1999/isj2-084/behan.htm

Ben-Ghiat, Ruth 2022, "The Return of Fascism in Italy", *The Atlantic*, 23 September. https://www.theatlantic.com/international/archive/2022/09/giorgia-meloni-italy-election-fascism-mussolini/671515/

Bonnel, Olivier 2023, "In Italy, Giorgia Meloni's government targets NGOs rescuing migrants at sea", *Le Monde*, 6 January. https://www.lemonde.fr/en/international/article/2023/01/06/in-italy-giorgia-meloni-s-government-targets-ngos-rescuing-migrants-at-sea_6010517_4.html

Bréville, Benoît 2023, "The Meloni Way", *Le Monde diplomatique*, July. https://mondediplo.com/2023/07/01edito

Broder, David 2022, "Italy's drift to the far right began long before the rise of Giorgia Meloni", *The Guardian*, 27 September. https://www.theguardian.com/commentisfree/2022/sep/26/italy-far-right-before-giorgia-meloni-berlusconi-brothers-of-italy

JASMINE DUFF

Review: Selling arms to anyone who wants them

Jasmine Duff is an organiser for the Campaign Against Racism and Fascism. She has also been involved in campaigning for Palestine, climate justice, and in organising Black Lives Matter rallies.

Antony Loewenstein, *The Palestine Laboratory. How Israel Exports the Technology of Occupation Around the World,* Scribe, 2023.

"War is hell but clearly it is good for business."
– Former chief lobbyist for pro-Israel US lobby group, AIPAC

A NTONY LOEWENSTEIN'S NEW BOOK *The Palestine Laboratory* is a forensic account of Israel's role in creating and distributing lethal weaponry and surveillance technology. He details how companies use the occupation of Palestine as a development lab, a testing ground, and a sales pitch for their deadly products. Loewenstein strips away the ideological trimmings that are used to hide Israel's true nature in mainstream discourse. He shows the reader that underneath all the talk of a "democracy in the Middle East" lies a brutal apartheid state which provides inspiration and arms to seemingly every despot under the sun. It's a safe bet, it turns out, that wherever you find a dictatorial, oppressive regime, Israel is probably selling them weapons. And it's not only weapons. The book describes the sickening developments in surveillance that Israel has sold to the world, with companies like NSO and Black Cube creating tools to access the most intimate details of people's lives through their phones.

The laboratory

Israel's existence is predicated on military domination over the Palestinian population. This has been the case since its founding in 1948. A stable and ever growing supply of weaponry has been key to maintaining and extending that dominance. From the 1930s, Zionists were building up an arsenal in Palestine. After 1939, Britain began military training for tens of thousands of Jews there. West German reparations from 1952 gave the fledgling Israeli state the investment to begin a weapons industry in earnest, and by the mid-1950s Israel's government-owned firms were selling weapons to other nations. The *modus operandi* was, in Loewenstein's words, "selling weapons to anybody who wants them" (p.17). Privately owned companies developed over the course of the next decade. Elbit systems, one of the most prominent firms, was founded in 1966, the year before the Six-Day War. By 1986, Thomas Friedman could write in the *New York Times* that "Israel, with only 4 million people, has become one of the top ten arms exporters in the world and Israeli businessmen are among the world's leading arms merchants" (p.26). The industry has expanded to over three hundred multinational companies and six thousand startups that employ hundreds of thousands of people. Israeli firms lead the field in invasive surveillance tech. The most famous example is cyber firm NSO Group, which developed the Pegasus phone-hacking software. Use of Pegasus is now nearly ubiquitous among governments worldwide. Countless journalists have ended up dead after it was used to hack their phones. The governments of India, Mexico, Saudi Arabia, Rwanda, Hungary and Morocco have all used it against critics or opposition politicians. Spanish authorities used it to spy on Catalan pro-independence politicians. Phone-hacking software built by Cellebrite, another Israeli cyber firm, was sold to Vladimir Putin's regime and has been used for years on dissidents.

Occupied Palestine is the perfect context in which to perfect murderous technology. Arms companies have an immediate field they can use to test their wares. Loewenstein documents how the recent

"Great March of Return", which gave hope to millions of supporters of Palestine, was used for this purpose. From 2018–19, thousands of Palestinians protested daily along Gaza's border, demanding the end of the Israeli blockade of Gaza and the right to return to the homes and land stolen from them. For Israel, it became "a lab and a showroom" (p.77). The state tested new weaponry on the march, including drone technology like the "Sea of Tears", which deployed tear gas, and "skunk water", a foul-smelling liquid emitted from a water cannon. Drones were also used to transmit messages to protesters, including a message in Hebrew telling Jewish supporters not to "stand with the enemy".

The occupation also serves as a sales pitch. Former South African politician Andrew Feinstein recounted to Loewenstein his experience of attending the Paris Air Show in 2009. In a luxury hotel, Israel's biggest weapons company, Elbit Systems, displayed a video of a target being assassinated by drone strike during a military operation in the occupied territories. As the video played, young saleswomen enthusiastically explained the technology to the crowd of generals and procurement officers. Feinstein later looked into the strike and discovered that the events depicted in the video had killed innocent Palestinians, including children. A minor detail. Each of the most deadly events in recent Palestinian history have been used as the equivalent of an expo. Weaponry used in the 2014 Gaza war was profiled (ie advertised) in international and domestic media, including bombs, tank shells and drones. Vladimir Putin rearmed Russia's surveillance system with Israeli drones, tried and tested in Gaza. These were used in Syrian President Bashar al-Assad's counter-revolutionary war.

Arming the world's despots

> "I don't care what the Gentiles do with the arms. The main thing
> is that the Jews profit."
> – Israeli adviser in Guatemala from the 1980s.

Loewenstein begins with an account of the 1973 Pinochet coup in Chile. The event is burned into the memory of the left because of the hopes held by the Chilean working class in the socialist government of

Salvador Allende, the advances in their consciousness and organisation as they fought against the CIA-backed coup, and the terror that the military dictatorship brought in its triumph. Thousands of socialists, communists and anarchists were tortured and killed by Pinochet's men in Estadio Chile. Loewenstein describes the life of Daniel, a man whose family fled to Israel after the coup. He recounts Daniel's horror upon discovering that Israel had helped the Pinochet dictatorship to rule, arming it with sophisticated weapons including missiles, tanks, and aircraft. Loewenstein quotes Eitan Kalinsky, sent to Chile in 1989 by the Jewish Agency for Israel. Kalinksy attended a protest against Pinochet and watched streams of colour-changing water which pushed back the marchers and broke shop windows. The spray came from water cannons mounted on vehicles. "Look, it says Hakibbutz Haartzi Hashomer Hatzair," said a Hashomer Hatzair envoy watching with him. "We all knew it was made in Kibbutz Beit Alfa [in Northern Israel]," Kalinksy wrote.

Israel's backing for the Pinochet junta is part of a long-term pattern. The regime has developed and tested its weapons on Palestinians, and then sold them to despots across the world who seek to carry out similar terror on their own populations. Loewenstein argues that 1967 marked an important turning point in Israel's international relationships. "Before the Six Day War," he argues, "Israeli policy was not noble but at least gave the rhetorical impression of (sometimes) opposing repression" (p. 32). After the Six Day War, Israel's relationships with right-wing despots strengthened, multiplied and became more public. Israel has long been referred to as America's watchdog in the Middle East, and maintains a close relationship with the United States, while putting its own interests first. By partnering with Israel, including in more ordinary trade, regimes not only acquire arms, but hope to build closer ties with Washington.

Indonesia is a good example. In 1967, the Suharto regime took power of the country following a mass slaughter of communists and anyone who could be smeared as such. Half a million people were murdered. Israel's national intelligence agency Mossad began a close trade relationship with the new regime, involving beef, corn, oil and cotton production. During the 1994 Rwandan genocide, Israel shipped weapons including Uzi submachine guns and hand grenades to the Hutu regime, which killed around 800,000 Tutsis in 100 days. Israel has armed the repressive South Sudanese regime, and sold military equipment to the genocidal junta in Myanmar until at least 2018.

Yet Israel's favourite dictators tend to be based in Latin America. Israel provided weapons and advice to US-backed right-wing death squads in Nicaragua, Honduras, El Salvador and Panama. Following a CIA-backed coup in Guatemala in 1954, the country had a succession of repressive right-wing governments. Between 1960 and 1996, roughly 200,000 people were killed in a civil war. Israel had a particularly close relationship with Guatemalan President Efrain Ríos Montt, who killed up to 75,000 people during his rule from 1982 to 1983. Israeli military advisors assisted him in his coup, and Ríos himself attributed part of his success to the fact that his soldiers were trained by the Israelis (p.40).

Today, Israel continues to assist and inspire right-wing despots. The regime of Narendra Modi in India has used Israel's occupation of Palestine as an example in its own occupation of Kashmir. In 2019, India's consul general in New York, Sandeep Chakravorty, said: "we already have a model in the world... If the Israeli people can do it, we can also do it" (p.126). And it goes beyond just inspiration. India was Israel's biggest weapons export market from 2015 to 2020, filling 43 percent of total sales. Lowenstein rightly argues that the two countries are linked by a mutual embrace of ethno-nationalism, and a material relationship built on defence exchange.

Israel and the migrant crisis

Israel has created one of the world's biggest ongoing refugee crises by carrying out mass expulsions of Palestinians from their homes and by turning Palestine into a war zone. But it has also played an important role in the militarisation of the European Union's borders. In 2020, the EU announced US$91 million in partnerships with Israeli weapons firms to run a drone presence over the Mediterranean. The drones are part of the rapidly expanding web of Frontex, the EU agency responsible for keeping refugees out. According to Loewenstein, Frontex is alerted to the presence of refugee boats by Israeli drones. It then often feeds the coordinates to the Libyan coastguard, known for being the most brutal and inhumane of all of the national coastguards, to intercept. Between 2014 and publication of Loewenstein's book, 22,784 people died in the Mediterranean. Frontex has grown from having 45 employees in 2005 to over 2,000 today. It has proposed a staff of 10,000 by 2027,[1] and met with 108 defence companies including Israeli firms 17 times between 2017 and 2019. Israeli surveillance firm Cellebrite provides Frontex with technology to spy on asylum seekers by getting into their smartphones, and Greece and Cyprus have conducted naval drills in the Mediterranean with Israel. In 2021, the *Guardian* reported that Services Australia had paid A$1.2 million to Cellebrite to obtain data from the phones of welfare recipients.[2]

What now?

Given what comes before, Loewenstein's conclusion seems somewhat incongruous. He places at least a vague hope in court cases, the UN and hypothetical Israeli liberal values in finding a solution to the crisis in Occupied Palestine. He writes:

> Israel and its supporters must make a choice between their commitment to Zionism and adherence to liberal values. It's impossible to continue to believe in both, considering the state of apartheid across both Israel and Palestine. (p.214)

Israel has never adhered to liberal values. The Zionism of the state has been based upon violent barbarism since its inception. But this final chapter is offset by the scathing criticism which fills the rest of the book, which accurately presents a picture of a despotic, sprawling arms industry working hand in glove with the Israeli state, the US, the European Union, and a plethora of dictatorships and despots.

Loewenstein writes that "The need for Israelis and Palestinians to live together in peace has long been obvious, but mostly dismissed as unrealistic by opponents" (p.211). But a two-state solution, which envisages Israel and a Palestinian state coexisting in peace, is a fantasy.[3]

---

1.   European Parliament 2019.
2.   Taylor 2021.
3.   For a more in-depth argument, see Fox 2020.

It always has been. The various US-sponsored so-called peace processes carried out over decades have made this clear. From the Camp David Accords of 1978 to the Oslo Accords which concluded in 1995, all of the various "peace" schemes have only bolstered Israel's power.

Recent developments make the utopianism of this position even clearer. Israel is currently defined as the nation-state of the Jewish people rather than of its citizens, leaving its non-Jewish residents to sit at the back of the bus. This is just one manifestation of a process whereby hard and far-right politics increasingly dominate every aspect of official Israeli society. The right has triumphed in all five elections between 2019 and 2022, with parties competing over who could promise the most bombings and annexations. The current Israeli government is the most right-wing in history, one in which open fascists participate alongside religious zealots and other hard-right figures. Loewenstein aptly describes Netanyahu's re-election in 2022 as "the equivalent of the KKK breaking down the door brandishing an assault weapon"(p.211). The anti-democratic judicial reform passed into law in July, which gives the government even more freedom to expand settlements, is just the latest expression of the natural trajectory of a state based on dispossession and domination.

Loewenstein can hardly be blamed for not offering a clearer path forward. The situation is desperate. The Arab states are increasingly abandoning even feigned backing for Palestine, and there hasn't been a mass revival of civil resistance since the 2021 Unity Intifada. Despite this, the widespread protests and nationwide strike of the Unity Intifada show the possibility for mass resistance, as did the revolutions that swept the region in 2011 and 2019.

Despite this minor criticism, Loewenstein's book is an important weapon in the struggle against Israel's occupation of Palestine, and indeed the very existence of Israel as an ethno-nationalist state. It should be read by all those with an interest in the struggle for justice and the debauched dealings of international weapons companies.

References

European Parliament 2019, Press release: "EU Border and Coast Guard Agency: 10 000 operational staff by 2027", 28 March. https://www.europarl.europa.eu/news/en/press-room/20190327IPR33413/eu-border-and-coast-guard-agency-10-000-operational-staff-by-2027

Fox, Vashti 2020, *The Story of Palestine*, Red Flag Books.

Taylor, Josh 2021, "Services Australia pays \$1.2m for controversial spyware for fraud investigations", *The Guardian*, 14 October. https://amp.theguardian.com/australia-news/2021/oct/14/services-australia-pays-12m-for-controversial-spyware-for-investigations

ANNEKE DEMANUELE

Review: Retelling race and critiquing identity politics

Anneke Demanuele is the national convenor of University Students for Climate Justice, and has also been involved in campaigns against the far right, for refugee rights and against attacks on education.

Kenan Malik, *Not So Black and White: A History of Race from White Supremacy to Identity Politics,* Hurst, 2023.

"White freedom". "Black betrayal". "Stay in your lane". To be antiracist in the twenty-first century is to view political values in racial terms; to insist that if one is reactionary, one has lost the privilege of being black; to erect racial boundaries beyond which certain people should not step. Where once anti-racists might have seen these as prescriptions to challenge, now they are regarded as edicts to embrace. And where once antiracists saw their mission as combating racism, now many see it as confronting whiteness. (p.236)

IN *NOT SO BLACK AND WHITE,* Kenan Malik puts forward a radical challenge to the identity politics that dominates the left and asks how such a defeatist and dangerous worldview arose. In doing so he explores the roots of race as a category and the purpose for which it was developed. Malik shows that race is a decidedly modern concept. He also shows that far from being a politics rooted in left-wing traditions, identity politics has its origins in the construction of race as a category itself, that is, it actually has its theoretical origins in the racist right.

Malik instead wants progressive, anti-racist politics to revive the approach he believes typifies the radical Enlightenment period – universalism. This is the idea that all people share a common humanity, that people are born equal, and that they should have equal rights.

Malik's book is a genuinely exciting and stimulating work, one that hums with rage at the injustice of our modern society. He wants to revive the traditions of working-class militancy and solidarity to overcome this. There are limitations to the book; importantly it lacks a discussion of what social transformation will be needed to overcome racism and oppression, and has an almost uncritical analysis of radical liberalism. Despite these deficiencies, Malik's book is still a valuable read for radicals who want to understand why racism persists today, and for the discussion of identity politics.

There are four narratives running through *Not So Black and White*. First, there is a retelling of the story of race (p.4). Second, Malik points to the powerful resistance movements against racism and colonialism and shows how this resistance expanded the meaning of universality and inequality. The third narrative is the relationship between race and class, where Malik rightly argues that issues that seem straightforwardly about race can sometimes be best understood through the prism of class, and that "our preoccupation with race frequently hides the realities of injustice" (p.6). The final narrative of the book seeks to explain the emergence of modern identity politics.

The retelling of race

The most common understanding of racism relies on a conservative understanding of human nature, whereby humans are innately scared of "the other". According to this theory, we fear people who look different from us and therefore engage in racist behaviours based on more or less conscious racist ideas. This supposedly explains the full spectrum of racist behaviour: from derogatory language and exclusion of racially different people from certain spaces, right up to violent attacks, police killings and war. There also is a widespread acceptance of the idea that race is something fixed and timeless, and this is linked to people's acceptance of racism as inevitable. In this view, the concept of race itself is never really challenged. In fact, it is largely assumed from the outset: "certain people are treated unequally because they belong to, or are seen as belonging to, a distinct race" (p.12). Malik helpfully points out that "the trouble with this argument is that race, like equality, is a social not a natural concept. It, too, had to be 'invented'" (p.12). Malik's book is an attempt to overturn all of these ideas, and discusses how they developed alongside modern capitalism. As part of this, he largely recapitulates the Marxist argument about the capitalist roots of modern racism, particularly in the slave trade.

As capitalism started to spread across the globe, it required vast swathes of territory and people in order to expand. That meant invasions, occupations and the stealing of people for slave industries. At the same time, the development of capitalism also meant the development of new ideas and ways of thinking. The bourgeois revolutions, aside from bringing a new ruling class to power, also created a revolutionary way of thinking about the world. Instead of there being a divine order, in which the king was the earthly representation of God and every man (and woman) had their position and station in life, we instead had "equality, liberty, fraternity"; the idea being that all men (for most Enlightenment thinkers, this did not include women) were equal.

To solve this contradiction between a system reliant on slavery and colonialism and the progressive republican ideal, race, racial categories and racism were developed. Where previously slaves from Africa and indentured servants from Ireland were often treated similarly, now a racialised hierarchy and set of laws and institutions had to be formed.

In the excellent chapter "The Invention of White Identity", Malik takes the reader through a history of the development of these new racial hierarchies.

> Transatlantic slavery did not develop for racial reasons. European elites would have developed a slave system utilizing poor whites had it been practically possible. Attitudes to black slaves and white servants were, in the seventeenth century, similar. Over time, though, slavery became racialized. Partly, this was for pragmatic reasons – slaves were cheaper and easier

to control. Partly, also, there developed deeper, more ideological motives. It was necessary to justify the acceptance of servitude in a society that proclaimed its fidelity to freedom and liberty. The racialization of slavery became a means of doing so. (p.70)

Malik sheds light on the faux science of race – including eugenics, phrenology, discussions of blood purity and intelligence tests – all of which attempted to give a rational and logical backing to what was a totally illogical idea: that humans from different places are inherently different, with some being superior and some being inferior. Malik writes of these scientists and thinkers that "asking the questions 'how do we classify a race' and 'how many races are there'", led them down one of the "blindest alleys in modern science" (p.40).

It also gave rise to justifications for the worst horrors of the modern age. For instance, Malik rightly argues that Nazism and the policy of concentration camps were not an aberration but were developed out of practices drawn from other capitalist nations. In the chapter "Barbarism Comes Home", Malik rejects the idea that the Nazis or the Holocaust emerged from thin air: "they were made possible by the ideas of race that had become deeply rooted in Western societies and by the practices of colonialism" (p.117). He also shows that much of the precedent for the categorisation of races and a legal framework for this was drawn by the Nazis from the United States. "Nazi lawyers, James Q. Whitman notes in his study of American influence on Nazi racial jurisprudence, 'regarded America, not without reason, as the innovative world leader in the creation of racist law'" (p.130).

Malik draws these connections and links, not to take away from the absolute barbarism of the Holocaust, but to show that:

> Nazis drew upon pre-existing cultural attitudes and practices; that ideas about extermination and about "who should and should not inhabit the world" were commonplace in discussions of colonialism and "primitive peoples". If we fail to recognize this, we not only entrench historical amnesia about colonialism but also face the jeopardy of normalizing colonial behaviour and attitudes. (p.139)

Of course, even when slavery was defeated through revolutionary struggles and social movements, racism did not disappear. It has continued to serve useful functions for the capitalist and ruling classes and remains deeply embedded in society. Black and brown people can be paid less than their white counterparts, forced into jobs and conditions that others won't accept, made into scapegoats, and subjected to racist prejudice and abuse. However, identifying the origins of all these complex and contradictory processes is vital, both to reassert a materialist understanding of oppression and to point to the need to overthrow capitalism to end it.

Racism, colonialism and resistance

Malik argues that many anti-racists now dismiss the Enlightenment, including its universalism and rationalism, as Eurocentric, racist or conservative. But in contrast to this popular reading, Malik insists that for all its limits, the Enlightenment was given meaning through the struggles of oppressed and colonised people, and that its ideals inspired resistance among those who were oppressed.

To flesh out this argument Malik draws on the revolutionary experience of Toussaint Louverture and the Haitian revolution. He argues that this was the third great Enlightenment revolution, following the French and the American revolutions (p.141). The Haitians also took the meaning of the Enlightenment further than their European counterparts and imbued it with new meaning. Where Enlightenment thinkers fused ideas of universalism with a cynical defence of slavery, the Haitian rebels were the first to truly champion justice for all. In doing so, they transformed the meaning of universalism and resolved one of the key contradictions of the Enlightenment (p.142). Malik recounts a story about slaves who had risen up against their masters and burned down buildings:

> Just one building was left standing, in which had lived the insurgents' commander. Inside, on a mahogany table, he had placed the single book that had survived the incineration of Leclerc's library – Raynal and Diderot's *Histoire des Deux Indes*. It

was open on the page that warned of the "terrible reprisals" that colonists would face if slaves were not emancipated.

It was revolutionary trolling at its best. It is also a reminder of the complex relationship between the radicalism of the Enlightenment and the obscenity of slavery, of both the willingness of French revolutionaries to maintain human bondage and the inspiration that Enlightenment writing could provide for slave insurrectionists. (p.143)

Malik wants readers to remember this relationship between the radical Enlightenment ideals and the racially oppressed. Discussing CLR James's writings on the Haitian revolution, Malik writes:

Louverture was significant to James not just because he had led the first great slave revolution; it was also that in so doing, he had made concrete the distinction between the immorality of European colonialism and the moral necessity of the ideas that flowed out of the Enlightenment. Most importantly for James, Louverture had shown how a struggle for emancipation could transform the meaning of universalism. (p.154)

More broadly, discussions of the Enlightenment and Enlightenment values are central to the overall argument in the book. In discussing the shifts made through the Enlightenment period, Malik writes: "Over the following century, nature, not God, would come to sanctify the placing of 'men in different stations'. Why did different peoples occupy different places in the social hierarchy? Because they were naturally – racially – different" (p.29).

Malik argues that there are two strands to the Enlightenment and universalism – the liberal and the radical. He rightly points out that some of the most influential Enlightenment thinkers, such as Hume, Kant and Jefferson, combined "a defence of liberty and equality with profoundly racist ideas". But others, such as Diderot, represent a radical strand that strove to "tear the old house of *ancien régime* society down and put another in its place" (p.24). These thinkers drew on the actions of revolutionaries such as the Levellers, which they believed could actually "make good" on the claims of the Enlightenment. They realised that to do so would require a fundamental transformation of society.

So tension developed within the Enlightenment, and through the broader transformations going on at the time. Would the bourgeois revolutions end with a codifying of social differences masked by a rhetoric of equality, or would the ideas of the Enlightenment be pushed to their logical extreme? Malik sees current debates about race and identity as similar to those that played out in the Enlightenment. His central claim is that we need to return to the best of the Enlightenment's universal ideals to confront racial oppression.

But this raises a key weakness of the book, which is that Malik is fairly uncritical of classical liberal ideas. There's a reason why the ideas of equality and fraternity were important for the emerging bourgeoisie. They were needed to justify the abolition of the rigid hierarchy of the feudal era, to allow them to climb up the class ladder and emerge as a new ruling class.

Malik's views echo those of the modernist writer Marshall Berman, who was similarly hostile to contemporary politics' dismissal of the universal ideals of the Enlightenment:

> Post-modernists maintain that the horizon of modernity is closed, its energies exhausted – in effect, that modernism is *passé*. Post-modernist social thought pours scorn on all the collective hopes for moral and social progress, for personal freedom and public happiness, that were bequeathed to us by the modernists of the eighteenth century Enlightenment. These hopes, post-modernists say, have been shown to be bankrupt, at best vain and futile fantasies, at worst engines of domination and monstrous enslavement.[1]

Both Malik and Bermann bristle at the way that postmodernists, or for Malik, Identitarians, reject modernism and Enlightenment thinking.

---

1. Berman 1988, p.9.

But radicals and anti-racists need to go beyond the Enlightenment, building on its best elements while transcending its inherent limitations. For this project, Marx is a better guide than Malik and Berman, in that he abandons radical liberalism in favour of a perspective that is rooted in the class struggle, and sees the liberation of humanity tied up in the project of working-class self-emancipation. As capitalism has developed, and the working class has established itself as the largest class, a collective class, and one that tends towards struggle, Marx was right to say that the only road to a universal humanism runs through working-class revolution. This class is the only one that is capable of transforming society and overcoming both class and oppression.

Race and class

"Racial ideology was the inevitable product of the persistence of differences of rank, class and peoples in a society that had accepted the concept of equality." (p.50)

To give Malik some credit, however, he is far stronger on the question of class than most writers today. Throughout the book, Malik emphasises the close relationship between race and class and the way one's class position informs one's experience of racial oppression. He also makes the useful point that some questions that are usually understood as issues of race are actually laden with questions of class.

To point to how we could overcome the "sharp end of racism", Malik excavates the history of united working-class struggles against racism. He cites a number of examples, such as the trial of the Scottsboro boys, which was dismissed as unimportant by the middle-class NAACP. While the NAACP abandoned the Scottsboro boys to their deaths, the Communist Party fought for their freedom. It was the Communists, white and Black, who organised Black sharecroppers and the unemployed. Malik retells the important history of civil rights unionism which challenged colour bars, struggled for equal pay and campaigned against segregation through the Great Depression onwards. He shows how "as blacks organised side-by-side as equals 'the aura of naturalness and inevitability that surrounded segregation' cracked" (p.210).

In thinking about the creation of race and class, it is useful to consider that as much as the categories of Black and Asian had to be created, the category of white had to be as well. Here questions of race and class are again relevant. The construction of a cross-class white identity took different routes in America and Britain. It was only with the racialisation of slavery that a cross-class "white identity" was really constructed in America. After that process took place, there was a desire to keep white blood "pure", and so things such as discriminatory immigration practices, sterilisation and the like took hold. The issue remained fiercely contested, so Irish immigrants in the nineteenth century were basically seen as Black. Only when the fear-mongering about Irish immigration subsided were they able to be subsumed into the category of white. Malik explains this by arguing that the question of whiteness was "constructed as much out of fear as out of self-regard" (p.65). Having white or Irish workers and indentured slaves identify with Black slaves and workers would have presented a problem of class resistance to their rule. The creation of a white identity created a cross-class identification that, while false, could incorporate white workers ideologically, while separating them from their class comrades.

Compared to the development of a white identity in America, the situation in Victorian-era Britain was quite different. There it was the working class who were seen as a "distinct breed", and social status was in many ways more fundamental to social position than skin colour (p.79). Malik shows how those who protested against the injustices of the emerging capitalist system were described as "negroes" (p.83). But as capitalism and colonialism developed, a cross-class white identity again had to be forged, and by the second half of the nineteenth century, white skin became an "essential mark of a gentleman" (p.85).

What Malik does well is show that race had to be constructed both in terms of whiteness and Blackness and that who fitted into which category could shift according to the needs and interests of the ruling class. There is nothing fixed about race. Even today, racial categories are made and remade. One only has to think about the way Muslims from all ethnic backgrounds were collectively racialised during the War on Terror, or the changing experience and identity of Greek and Italian migrants in Australia. Malik is also refreshingly insistent that any tendency for white workers to identify with the white ruling class is a false one, and does not serve their best interests.

Malik wants us to rediscover the history of working-class struggles against oppression in order to move past the pessimism of modern racial politics. These politics assume that we can never overcome racism, and the best we can achieve is a recognition of mutually antagonistic identities. Malik persuasively argues that working-class struggle can actually overcome the oppression people face. This argument is the bridge back to his earlier attempt to salvage the universalism of the Enlightenment. Malik thinks that we should fight to overcome racism, and "transcend the concept of race", and to do this would require a "social revolution" (p.293).

But although Malik argues that we need "not just an intellectual revolution, but a social one too", it's never spelled out what this revolution will look like, what social force will lead it, and what type of society would be built after it. Though much of the book is spent talking about the necessity of cross-racial working-class struggle, Malik never really argues that such struggles have the capacity to overcome capitalism. It's also not clear what Malik thinks will lead to the social revolution he argues for. For that, a reader would best refer to Marxist classics on the topic, which make the case for working-class universalism while also defending the need to address specific grievances for racial minorities and other oppressed groups.

Identity politics

The last section of Malik's book deals with the question of identity politics, which is the lens through which much of the left, both in academic and activist circles, view the world.

Identity politics adopts a fundamentally pessimistic worldview, one that sees racism, sexism and every other form of oppression as innate and eternal. It follows from this that the struggle against these oppressions, while admirable, is foredoomed to failure. The political horizons are narrowed; no matter how much we'd like, we can never really overcome oppression. Instead, we should highlight the marginalisation of oppressed groups and make people aware of their unconscious biases and micro-aggressions. Identity politics fractures the oppressed into smaller categories, rather than looking for commonalities between oppressed peoples and asking how could we end that oppression. This is a set of politics that says only someone who has a specific experience of identity or oppression can talk on that issue, and that there's a hierarchy of oppressions and identities. If you are lucky enough not to be on the bottom of that pile, you actively engage in and benefit from the oppression of those below you.

One of the interesting arguments made in *Not So Black and White* is that the modern identity politics of today have roots in the conservative politics of the past. Against radical universalism, conservatives argued that human beings should be reduced to cultural backgrounds, that one's identity was linked to one's race, and that you had to protect racial and cultural groups from dilution (for example via eugenics or segregation).

Today, the political right *and* left prosecute the argument that cultural groupings should remain distinct from one another. Many will be familiar with the claims of cultural appropriation made by much of the online and liberal left today. Malik posits that what the left and right have in common, by segmenting the population into cultural and identity-based groups, is a "hostility to universalism, a rejection of Enlightenment ideals as simultaneously ethnocentric, the product of European culture, and insufficiently ethnocentric, steamrollering cultural differences to impose a universalist perspective" (p.288). It should come as no surprise then that the political right are happy to employ politics of identity.

> Most conservative critics of identity politics are not opposed to identity politics, just to the identity politics of the left. They despise Black Lives Matter for its "racism" and condemn the divisiveness of a concept such as "white privilege". But they want to keep London (and Paris and Berlin) primarily white and to protect the European homeland from being colonized by marauding immigrants. All of which takes us to the deeper problem with the mainstream right's embrace of white identity. The reactionary right – Nouvelle Droite, Generation Identity, the

> alt-right in America – uses the language of diversity and identity
> as a means of rebranding racism. (p.285)

However, it's not the case that the conservative right totally rejects Enlightenment ideas. They can and do use them to pursue racist talking points and justify forms of social inequality. Often they will talk about "not seeing race" or being "colourblind" in order to paper over the real oppression racial groups face. As well, countries like Australia have used official policies of "multiculturalism" in order to more subtly assimilate people into "Australian" capitalism and nationalism. Further, the right doesn't only employ identity politics, they attack and lambast the left for its identity politics, with their current obsession with "woke culture" being the clearest example.

So any real assessment of the situation suggests that both the Enlightenment and a rejection of it can justify racism. This goes against Malik's claim that those who reject the Enlightenment are conservative (left-wing identitarians included) and those who embrace it are progressive.

In discussing the question of left-wing variants of identity politics, Malik also takes a fresh look at the development of the Black Lives Matter movement in the United States. Using recent studies, Malik demonstrates that "police violence is correlated with poverty – the poorer a neighbourhood, the greater the risk of an individual being killed by the police. African Americans are disproportionately poor and working class; poverty and class location must also play a role in their being victims of police violence" (p.227). This argument is not made in order to downgrade the importance of the Black Lives Matter movement, or the centrality of racism to the construction and maintenance of inequality in the US. But without incorporating both race and class, it is harder to understand why police target specific Black communities, and harder to build coalitions with other workers and poor people who have an interest in fighting back together.

Oppressed groups are not homogeneous. Like every community, the oppressed are internally divided on all sorts of lines, the most important being class. Jay Z is not in danger of being stopped and frisked, nor will Beyonce ever need to work as a domestic servant to pay the bills. Malik writes:

> There is no single identity or set of interests that bind together all black people, and only black people; still less, all people of colour... To assume that there is only reinforces the power of the black elites and diminishes the voices of black workers, making it more difficult to tackle the problems facing those at the sharp end of racism. (pp.223–4)

Malik's arguments against identity politics are important ones, and largely valid. However, sometimes they verge on one-sidedness. It is true that it will take a working-class struggle to overcome oppression, but movements against particular forms of oppression can be vital beginnings for these types of moments, and such movements will often start with a focus on issues that affect a minority. As well, many people joining the left take the language of identity for granted, and so socialists need to patiently explain the limitations of these ideas, and try to win those concerned with oppression to a working-class and anti-capitalist perspective.

It is also important to remember that our key enemies are the right and the reactionary racists, not those on the left who sometimes get things wrong. We can have debates and comradely disagreements, but our ire should be directed towards those who want to maintain and strengthen the racist institutions in our society. Debate on the left is necessary though, because our understanding of where racism developed from, who benefits and how we overcome it will be central to a successful anti-racist struggle. Malik's book is a really useful contribution to that sort of discussion.

Reference

Berman, Marshall 1988, *All That's Solid Melts to Air,* Penguin Books, New York.